NO MORE LONELY NIGHTS

Also by
Susan Price, M.S.W.

THE FEMALE EGO

NO MORE LONELY NIGHTS

Overcoming the Hidden Fears that
Keep You from Getting Married

Dr. Stephen Price
and
Susan Price, M.S.W.

G. P. PUTNAM'S SONS   NEW YORK

G. P. Putnam's Sons
Publishers Since 1838
200 Madison Avenue
New York, NY 10016

Library of Congress Cataloging-in-Publication Data

Price, Stephen.
No more lonely nights.

1. Love.   2. Interpersonal relations.   3. Mate
selection—United States.   4. Marriage—United States.
I. Price, Susan, date.   II. Title.
HQ801.P895   1987   306.8'1   87-7223
ISBN 0-399-13306-2

Printed in the United States of America
1   2   3   4   5   6   7   8   9   10

ACKNOWLEDGMENTS

We are grateful to many people whose influence, support and assistance have contributed to the development of this book.

Our friends and family have revealed through the examples of their own lives how to make marriage work: the Johnsons: Lois and Herb, Jeff and Ellen, Steve and Karen; the Prices: Bob and Jane, Virginia and Peter Enemark, Tim and Cindy; Violet and Lyle Fitch; Helen and Vincent La Selva.

Our many wonderful teachers: the faculty at the Institutes of Religion and Health; also Louis Birner, Mary Bolton, John Kildahl, Richard Erskine, Laura Perls, Rebecca Trautmann, Wilbert Sykes.

Our good friends and colleagues: Sandra Mignott, Pat Hill, Jim Kousoulas, Marla Mandis, Elaine Peterson, Linda Fitch; the Staff Directors at the Counseling and Human Development Center in New York City: Beverly Musgrave, Alan Chisholm, Kim Jones, Mary Ragan, Fred Turpin; Tom Bowers, Andrew Mullins, and Bruce Forbes of St. Bartholomew's Church in New York City.

Our children who are our great inspiration: Angela and Michael Price.

We wish to thank Philippa Brophy, our dedicated agent. Thanks also to Christine Sweeney for her assistance, and to Mary Kurtz for her insightful and careful copy editing. Special thanks to Chris Schillig, masterful editor, whose help along the way has been invaluable.

*This book is dedicated with gratitude
to our many patients who have taught
us so much.*

CONTENTS

BEFORE YOU READ
THIS BOOK

All of us have hidden fears about loving and getting close to someone. These fears are reactions to painful experiences of early childhood and development that are so upsetting we repress or forget them as a way of dealing with them. But the original fears, now hidden, continue to influence us in the present. As adults, we may find ourselves resistant to getting deeply involved with someone, or to getting married. This resistance is a protection; it is a defensive wall we erect to quiet the hidden fears in our unconscious. But when unconscious fears are operating, we don't realize what is happening, and what we don't know *can* hurt us.

There are other kinds of hidden fears that are not necessarily related to deep-seated psychological pain. These fears come out of observing friends or relatives who must deal with the complexities of love and marriage, or of having had the experience of a bad marriage yourself at one time. How many people do you know who have happy marriages? Being dependent upon someone you can't directly control can make you want to shy away, especially when you observe others having difficulties in their marriages. We have been told innumerable times by women patients that they don't see how they can possibly be married *and* maintain a sense of fulfillment as individuals. Such women are being held back by natural fears about the consequences of mating.

We are two psychotherapists who work every day with people who are identifying these hidden fears and learning how to overcome the resistance to mating. We help women develop the consciousness and skills to protect themselves while growing in their ability to be close and be married. And because we also are married to each other, we have dealt with these same hidden fears and resistances in our own relationship.

It is sometimes difficult to believe the automatic and powerful control that unconscious fear can have in your life. A woman under the spell of fear is often confused as to why she is single, remaining blind to the depth of her fear of love. She may have no idea that fear is running—and ruining—her love life, or she may not know what to do about it.

We believe the answer to loneliness is understanding and overcoming your hidden fears. This is a very personal enterprise, because each woman has her own history and experience that may have caused her to be fearful. We hope you will be able to identify with the contents of this book, and that it will help you along your journey of overcoming the fears that keep you from getting married. Take your time in reading this material, and know that you are not alone in your loneliness. Most important, have hope that if you really open yourself to the task of self-awareness, fear can lose its power to keep you lonely.

In order to get married, you must be honest about your own loneliness, and your need for love. This crucial discovery steers you away from the wrong choices of partners. When you are truly available for love, you will not cling to a man who treats you badly. When you are ready for commitment, you will not be attracted to a man who is distant, but will seek simple, private experiences of intimacy with a man. We will offer insight along the way about how good relationships work, so that you will know how to look for the comfort and closeness you need.

A woman who admits her desire for love and is not afraid of it can beat the statistics and find a loving partner at any age. To be married today, you must be willing to put energy into pioneering the new marriage relationship between equal partners. Mating is always difficult to accomplish, and it is especially difficult today. But you are not alone in your longing for committed love, and a life lived with the comfort of that love. When you are ready psychologically, you *can* find—and marry—a loving man.

·1·
A CRISIS IN LOVING

This is a very difficult time in history for you to be seeking a marriage relationship. Like many single women, you have probably been earnestly involved in creating your own life as an individual. Marriage has not been the first priority in your life, and you have been focused instead upon career development. And like many other women, you have discovered that the "temporary single person" lifestyle you created until Mr. Right came along is now a permanent way of life.

Single Is Lonely

Life without a partner has its own wholeness: There are the day-to-day routines of work, paying bills, taking vacations, having pets and sending Christmas cards. Yet what were once the family activities of your childhood are now solitary ones.

A Crisis in Loving

The women we see in therapy often express a painful realization that the independence they embraced in order to develop themselves is no longer exciting or fulfilling. They tell us that an independent lifestyle feels like a lonely prison. They are free to manage their time, but they are not free to be intimate. They are free to go on interesting vacations, but they are not free to share them. They are free to make exciting career moves, but they do not feel free to get married.

Many women are living in a state of chronic loneliness. Indeed, therapists view this as a major mental health problem today. When you are caught up in the dating cycles of the singles world, the marriage of your parents may seem passé, and yet your need for a traditional loving commitment cannot easily be denied. Cycles of disappointing relationships condition you to compulsively avoid the risk of ever being hurt again. But in playing it safe, you don't allow yourself to be available for the possibility of genuine love in your life.

A crisis in relationships has occurred. Women cry out to friends, to therapists, to themselves: "I've waited too long!" If you aren't married by thirty or if you haven't stayed with an early marriage you may feel that it's impossible to create long-term closeness, to have children, or to find anybody at all at this late date.

You may be looking back in regret, realizing that the best time and place to meet a partner was probably in college. The senior-year panic has been transferred to age thirty-five, a point at which twenty-eight percent of women can no longer conceive a child. Despair takes over as a woman approaches forty and the percentage of those unable to conceive is up to a shocking sixty-eight percent. "The feminists never told me that I would be unfulfilled by my 'successful' career at forty," lamented one such woman, "or that I would feel so lonely."

The need to love and be loved doesn't go away just because you have become self-actualized in your work. Becoming self-sufficient and self-assertive doesn't fill your emotional reservoirs. Getting rid of a relationship that wasn't working doesn't mean that you don't need a deep relationship. If you're feeling desperately unhappy about being single, you're probably suffering from profound love deprivation. Your normal human emotional hungers and needs haven't been satisfied, and your extreme neediness can be causing severe depression.

Without the emotional constancy that marriage provides, the events of your life won't be fully affirmed. Important experiences such as celebrating a success or mourning a loss tend to get short-circuited without an intimate partner with whom you can share it all. You feel lonely because many aspects of living are emotionally incomplete without the dialogue that helps you to work through your experiences. Sharing them with a partner gives you perspective, which helps you put certain matters to rest and continue to move forward. When your life becomes a monologue rather than a dialogue, you are starved for affection and will have problems moving ahead.

When you are suffering from lack of affection, you may feel the intensity of your unmet needs, but you may not realize that what you are needing is something very basic, like your need for oxygen or food. The most simple gestures of human recognition—saying "Pass the butter" at breakfast, mumbling "Good night," having a warm body to lean on in front of the television—remind us that we exist and let us know we are nice to be with. The comforting presence of a partner is deeply affirming because it is a reliable and familiar source of attention.

Lack of intimacy can lead to deep loneliness, and you may not realize that what you need are small but valuable gestures of human warmth. A needy woman gets on the wrong track when she looks for an intense sexual experience to satisfy her desperate desire for loving attention. The intensity of her neediness distorts her understanding of what she needs—kindness and attentive listening from a man. Simple, good company will nurture her spirits, not a torrid love affair. As a wise friend once put it, "What makes for an exciting novel makes for terrible living." Don't let your loneliness lead you to seek stimulation instead of nurturance.

On the most basic level of all you need physical strokes. Dr. René Spitz, a psychiatrist studying hospitalized infants in the forties, discovered that those deprived of sufficient handling suffered depression and declining health. Even in adulthood, the most comforting form of stroking comes through physical intimacy. You may look for more subtle forms of recognition in your adult life, but the basic human desire to be touched and to experience intimacy on a childlike level is always with you.

The physical intimacies exchanged regularly by married partners continually fulfill these basic needs. A married woman may not sleep with the world's greatest lover, but she has a familiar, comforting man warming her sheets every night. The need to be loved is basic and constant, and it is difficult to meet that need without living in a marriage relationship.

The Price of Divorce

While some single women spent their twenties and thirties in self-development, many others spent those years struggling through or getting out of marriages that were not working. Maybe you found that an early marriage was wrong. Stifled in your personal growth, you had to find a way out before you suffocated or before despair destroyed your confidence in trying for success outside the relationship. Although you once made your marriage a high priority, you ended up putting primary value on getting out of it. The post-divorce healing process lasted for at least two years, and today you find yourself well established in your lifestyle as a single woman.

When you are lonely, you may remind yourself how precious your freedom is. The fear of being trapped is often stronger than your loneliness, and your joy at being released from that painful past marriage gives you surges of energetic delight in your singleness. You live on relief: no more being yelled at, no more trying to communicate with an "impossible" man, no more painful silences and impasses, no more fielding of criticism. It is such a relief to be released emotionally—from your guilt, rage or irritation at him, from feeling trapped and controlled by him or from excruciating boredom.

Many a divorced woman inwardly celebrates the absence of her mate. And yet, like the woman who has never married, she has experiences of extreme loneliness. Every woman needs to feel needed, to share intimacies, to be appreciated for those things only an intimate would notice. Even if you spent years extricating yourself from a relationship that wasn't working, you secretly wish you had a mate to satisfy the longing you now feel. Underneath the relief, desire persists: "If only I could find the right man and love him and have him love me back!"

Listening to the pain of women and sympathizing with their shock as the statistics on marriage and divorce are announced in the media are very important aspects of psychotherapists' work today. In this singles era, with the emphasis upon autonomy and freedom, it's shocking to realize that thousands of women of mating age don't feel they are free to get married. There is undoubtedly a crisis in relationships in our culture. Yet the way to respond to this mating crisis is to deal with your own personal crisis: What might *you* be doing to make intimacy with a man impossible? What attitudes are keeping *you* unavailable for marriage?

We believe you may unconsciously fear love.

Getting in Touch with Your Crisis in Loving

You can't begin to solve a problem without admitting to it, so you probably need to take a personal inventory of your own crisis in loving. And since loneliness can cast a pall of depression over you, it can make it difficult to focus on solving the problem. Answering this questionnaire is the first step in uncovering your inner conflicts about intimacy and mating.

1. Do you find yourself going in and out of relationships?
2. Has it been a long time since you were deeply involved with someone?
3. Are you involved in a relationship that isn't going anywhere?
4. Do you spend more time alone than you would like to?
5. Are you as happy about your personal life as you are about your work life?
6. Are your sexual relationships satisfying, or do you sense that something important is missing?
7. Do you expect to find the right man, or do you think that there are no prospects for you?
8. Are you still hurting from a former relationship?

Answer these questions as honestly as possible, and begin to focus on your inner fears about love and loving. The material in this book can help you make personal connections to the significant emotional events in your own life. Admitting to your present unhappiness is the first step to dealing with these key issues.

·2·
THE CULTURE USED TO HELP

It is important for you to know that *everyone* has hidden fears that work against getting married. Even if you had a wonderful and loving childhood without negative experiences that affected your ability to form loving relationships, you'll still have *natural* hidden fears of being controlled or overwhelmed by a close relationship, or the opposite fears: of being unloved, abandoned or not getting close enough.

The culture used to help us with these natural fears by prescribing forms and rituals for dating couples to go through. We didn't have to worry too much about getting too close because society demanded chaperones and forbade living together. Our fear of isolation and of not getting close enough was taken care of by the community's many opportunities for formal dates, involving families and matchmakers.

Thus the natural fears and ambivalences of single

people were answered formerly by the larger community and the accepted cultural patterns of mating. They made it easier for women, supporting them and helping to usher them into marriage by a variety of traditions responsive to their fears.

One of the reasons you are now single and confused may well be that many of these cultural traditions no longer exist. You're on your own in a fearful arena.

The Relationship Revolution

It seems as if everything is viable today, that there are no rules or standards for relationships, courtship, marriage. The relationship revolution has destroyed both courtship rituals and traditional sexual roles, and a lot of men and women don't know how to get together. The relationship revolution has done what every revolution seeks to accomplish—create a complete and radical change in the way people live and relate to one another. Today, if you want to get married, you helplessly face a lack of structure governing relationships among adult singles.

Feminists, war protestors and advocates of sexual freedom wanted people to be in charge of their own destinies. The core belief was that people should decide what is right for themselves, an important corrective to earlier injustices. In the sixties men protested fighting and dying in a war they didn't support. Women resisted devoting their lives to husbands who wanted only domestic services, a job that prohibited them from developing their own talents. The destruction of the traditional marriage was supposed to free a woman to belong to herself, and conveyed the message to many women that independence meant freedom from male bondage.

When we dismantled the patriarchal marriage of the fifties—epitomized by *Father Knows Best*—we entered an era of experimentation. Not only did the sexual revolution influence the practices of single people, but the institution of marriage was weakened by the new permission to experiment. When we were in training to become psychotherapists, our monogamous lifestyle made us feel old-fashioned among our peers, most of whom were divorced singles. One of our supervisors in the early seventies recommended to all of his patients that they *not* get married. "Why do it when you don't have to? Live together!" he advised one and all, even though he himself was married. Today still we often hear reports from couples whose therapists advocate divorce after seeing them for only a few sessions. Things are bumpy between you? Split.

Because of the relationship revolution, the vacuum created by the loss of cultural and familial authority was soon filled by pseudo-therapeutic cults or religious and political organizers. In spite of the exhilaration generated by the openness to new freedoms, people began feeling vulnerable and hungry for structure—the very thing they had rebelled against since the sixties. Young people always need guidance, and many self-appointed gurus captured their allegiance. That's one of the reasons why cult membership is still popular today.

The relationship revolution of twenty years ago has left its mark: Many women still believe that marriage is "bad" for them. They don't want to be "just like their mothers." And they can't admit to wanting marriage deep down. To need love, in their eyes, is to be weak. To find it is to become enslaved again.

The Death of Courtship

In eras past, the beginning of love was carefully watched by the community, which insisted that romantic advances must imply commitment. Families and small communities shaped the mating rituals of young lovers, making sure that consummation came after the marriage vows. When we threw out the premarital sex taboo, we threw the baby out with the bath water: We overlooked the fact that its purpose went beyond hygiene, birth control or uptight morality. Waiting for sex was one way that the culture supported the blossoming of genuine love. The prescribed distance between couples provided the necessary psychological environment for courtship rituals to occur.

AMBIVALENCE IS NORMAL

Resistance to mating and intimacy has always been a problem for humans. In mating there is always a gradual buildup of advances and retreats in which the female who is desirous of mating may nevertheless reject her partner out of boredom or outright hostility. Resistance emanates from the part of the psyche that desires independence and control, that does not want to be dominated by another person. But through a series of rituals, her resistance is lowered and both partners finally give up control and succumb to their mating instincts. Variations on this scenario exist throughout the animal kingdom, and can help you understand that ambivalence is normal: The mating process invariably involves both a great sense of attraction and resistance toward the potential partner.

The post-fifties death of courtship was a serious blow to men and women seeking long-term partners. Courtship helps individuals overcome their innate resistance to mating. There is never an easy, ideal mating process, and the presence of hidden psychological fears makes it nearly impossible to mate. To understand how to get married, you must come to the realization that creating a bond with someone is a complex exercise in overcoming natural inner resistance. During courtship you discover the delights that are available with a partner, and through this process, you break down your resistance gradually, in a way that makes some loss of autonomy acceptable and indeed desirable.

THE WISDOM OF ELDERS

In the past the culture understood that resistance to mating is a fact of life, and it ushered young men and women through their resistances and into marriage. Today, however—for the first time in history—individuals are taking this enormous problem into their own hands. No wonder women don't feel free to mate: Culturally and historically mating has always been a community ritual.

One of the great truths about life is that you can only

understand it in hindsight. Looking back, you can see the things you should have done differently in order to get the outcome that you now wish you had. That's why the guidance of wise elders is so useful.

When a young man is joyfully "playing the field," he can't envision the prospect of reaching his twentieth wedding anniversary and finding himself inseparable from his wife. He doesn't know that in twenty years their love will be tamed into a deep affection that unites them until the grave.

A young career woman who wants her social life to imitate her fast-lane career can't imagine herself in twenty years with the quiet guy in the office who reads all the time. She doesn't know that he is the man who at fifty-five will bring her a rose from the garden with her morning coffee and comfort her with his love.

Looking at the older generation provides the true perspective on the meaning of marriage, and that generation once possessed influence and authority to help its children in the mating process. But in our youth-oriented culture, elders are quickly branded obsolete. As a result of our hard-won freedom from the influence of "stifling" tradition, we have few traditions left that can help us in forming mating relationships. Most women today find that their social life is vastly different from their parents'. They can't imagine the primary role that families once played in helping individuals get married, believing instead that any input from their parents is intrusive or irrelevant.

In close communities a generation ago, there was the advantage of knowing everyone in town and having a sense of everyone's family history. Parents expected certain standards for courting couples, and a woman was protected—not only sexually but also emotionally—from any behavior that was less than respectful. A dishonorable male didn't have access to self-respecting females in such tightly knit communities. Parents exerted gentle and sometimes not so gentle persuasion in guiding their sons and daughters toward the "right" mates. Maintaining the continuity of the marriage principle itself had a higher priority than finding an exciting partner. But the social upheaval of the last twenty years has created an unfathomable generation gap, and most parents keep their still strong conservative opinions to themselves.

The Post-Revolution Era

In the 1950s young men and women longed for sexual freedom and feared its immorality. Today the singles population is longing for love while fearing commitment. Some of the excesses of the singles scene have not been so much expressions of freedom as symptoms of depression. Casual sex and the use of stimulants doesn't satisfy the need for love, and love seems to be elusive and unattainable. Many people are deeply confused about what love is, and the phrase "making love" reveals this confusion; it usually means "making sex."

We are fulfilled by traditions that weave cords of permanence through our lives, and in order to have such fulfillment we must commit to particular, lifetime relationships. In maturity, we must realize the importance of narrowing options. Making choices allows us to experience a fulfilling sense of depth and permanence. Many single women think their chances of finding a partner are greater in a big city, but frequently this line of thinking doesn't actually lead to finding someone. The reason is that mating requires not expanding your possibilities but rather narrowing them to one person only, rejecting all other options.

If you are serious about wanting to marry you must reject the culture of the relationship revolution that says anything goes and all arrangements are subject to change. Marriage means opting for a final choice and committing yourself to it, though when you have been "free" for a long time, you may not like the idea of making a relationship compulsory rather than voluntary.

Even though there is considerable despair today among unmarried people who don't know how to establish permanent ties, we must appreciate the important reasons for breaking up relationship patterns of the past. Revolution is the way we give up rigid societal practices that don't benefit people. Our world has changed dramatically in the last twenty-five years, and relationships had to change to catch up with the times. It was of vital importance for people to free themselves from stultifying marriages, to explore new options, to ask the question: "What's in it for me?" However, these values in themselves are extreme and can lead to no marriage at all, to serial, open-option relationships and to self-absorbed narcissism.

In this post-revolutionary period the pendulum swings back toward the values of the past. We must rediscover the value of bonding. In order to form a close emotional attachment, there must exist commitment, equality and generosity between partners. Commitment makes it possible to cherish one special person and put great energy into that person. Equality means that both people have equal power in the relationship, and although their contributions may be different, they are equally valued. Generosity is the virtue that answers today's problem of excessive self-interest, which keeps people from bonding. Most marriage counselors would agree that the single most important quality in happy marriages is generosity. When couples experience the joys of giving and receiving in a committed and generous relationship, the answer to "What's in it for me?" will be clear. Plenty.

·3·
WOMEN WHO FEAR LOVE

At age thirty-five, Michelle was unhappy about being unmarried. An early marriage had ended in divorce, and Michelle went on to achieve some real career success as a fabric designer. Since age twenty-four she had participated in a series of relationships—some serious, some short-lived. Yet at thirty-five she had the uneasy feeling that she was not ready for marriage, even though she longed for it. Time and life experience had not really prepared her for mating. Instead her fears of getting close and staying close to a man had increased. She was confused when she tried to understand her relationship patterns, and felt like a failure. As lonely and needy as she felt, she was also wary and cynical about the possibilities of finding a real partner. In her first therapy session, Michelle burst into tears. "I'm sick of dating," she cried. "I've been dating for twenty years!"

Twenty-two-year-old Tara did not date at all. Her energy was divided between her job in an accounting firm and evening business courses. In her late teens she had had several sexual relationships with high school and college boys who were essentially drinking buddies. As a result of too many "after the party" depressions, she left college and got a job. Apart from her relationships with two girlfriends, she had become withdrawn socially. When Tara entered therapy she had not had a date for over eight months and was feeling a nagging loneliness. Although she had a fantasy of someday getting married and having children, she believed that in reality there was no man for her. The men her age were "immature," and the older ones were, of course, married.

At thirty-seven, Denise had never been married. Focused on career development, she had relinquished her only serious, long-term relationship years ago in favor of a two-year assignment abroad. When in the past six months an attractive and loving man became seriously interested in her, Denise began to feel threatened: His attentiveness awakened a deep longing for emotional closeness. At the same time she found herself pulling away, becoming strangely critical and disapproving of him. She entered therapy feeling successful in her career but uncomfortable about being unmarried, sensing that something important was missing in her life. Denise decided to explore her past history of avoiding committed relationships and to understand her ambivalence in wanting love yet rejecting the man in her life.

One Heartbreak Too Many: The Fear of Getting Hurt

These three women are patients in our practice. They are among the scores of unmarried women whom we have treated over the past fifteen years. Today, Michelle, Tara and Denise are all married after working through inner fears that were preventing them from making this commitment. In the early sessions each of these women complained about the difficulty of finding a suitable mate. But they were encouraged to focus primarily upon themselves, and to explore the hidden tendencies that might be holding them back from forming relationships. As different as Michelle, Tara and Denise are from one another, they shared a common problem: Each harbored deep fears of being hurt if they got close to a man. Each had understandable reasons for their fears, but the level of their distrust of men made it impossible for them to form intimate connections.

In examining the cases of many single women over the past fifteen years, we are convinced that the key psychological problem for single women who want to get married but can't is the fear of getting hurt. How many times can a woman tolerate the pain of being distanced from someone with whom she has felt a deep attachment? After experiencing a failed relationship, her fear of being hurt is so powerful that it prevents her from allowing closeness to occur again. Emotional heartbreak heals with a tough scar, and most people will not let themselves be hurt many times. Instead of yielding to love, they learn to question it with suspicion. Our experience has shown that people may stop loving after no more than two or three heartbreaks.

When Michelle probed her emotional history, she listed four serious heartbreaks—her father, her high school boyfriend, her husband and a live-in lover. She felt a strong need for a partner, but at the same time believed there was no possible way for her to be close to a man. Her history had well inoculated her against ever surrendering to love again.

Ask yourself about your own record of disappointments in love. How many times have you had to heal from a painful, failed relationship? If it's been more than twice, you will probably be deeply mistrustful of love.

When Tara examined her past experiences with men, she found them all distasteful. She admitted to feeling unconnected to her partners in sexual encounters, almost as if she had not been present. The young men she had partied with weren't interested in serious relationships, and Tara felt lonely after being with them. She didn't like men because they had never made her feel good about herself. Tara's fear of love was also connected to her pain over her parents' divorce when she was nine. After that trauma she felt distant from both parents as each became involved in new marriages.

When you look back to your own childhood, do you remember an absence of affection between you and your parents? Did you then tend to keep romantic relationships on a superficial basis, or have sex as a finale to a night of partying? If so, you probably expect intimacy to be unfulfilling.

Denise grew up with parents who believed that no boyfriend was good enough for her. Under their influence, she had rejected all close relationships with boys from an early age, even though this was painful. In therapy she discovered her fear of love stemmed from inexperience with men. She was highly competent in her work, but feared the feelings of incompetence that emerged whenever she was dating a man. She also became aware of harboring a fear of displeasing her parents by choosing the "wrong" man.

Have you, like Denise, developed yourself professionally but neglected to learn how to get your emotional needs met? Are you, like each of these women, inhibited by a fear of love and intimacy?

When there is fear of getting close, it is nearly impossible to mate. Without conquering your fears of love, you won't be able to make an intimate psychological connection with a prospective mate—even when he is available.

Many symptoms indicate a fear of love. One of them is excessive man-blaming. Another is a state of confused loneliness in which feelings of neediness make you shut down instead of reaching out to get your needs met. Fear of love also manifests itself in your choices of men: Intense longing for an unavailable, aloof man or having a relationship with a married man reveals an underlying fear of wholehearted closeness. Another symptom of your underlying fear of love can be excessive hype when you have a crush on a man. Overstimulation is a frequent coverup for anxiety or fear, and the high point on an emotional roller coaster inevitably descends to a depressing low.

These behaviors signal to others in many ways that you are not open to love, but you are probably unaware of them yourself. It is difficult to acknowledge that you are emotionally hooked on longing instead of on having a real relationship. When you spend a lot of time and energy wallowing in the pain of not having a man, the reason is fear. Secretly, you believe normal loving relationships are impossible. Though you may complain bitterly about being single, you are primed and ready to be disappointed in love.

Our suggestion to you that you may have unconscious fears of love is not an accusation. You have very good reasons for your fears of closeness. The issue is that you must deal with your fears and work them through rather than spend time blaming men or conditions in our society that make it difficult to mate. If your fears are crippling you, you won't connect with a man, even under ideal conditions. Therefore your initial focus must be on the attitudes within yourself that are keeping you from getting close. You are the only person that you can work on, and you'll probably discover that there is much useful work to be done in understanding yourself and your inner attitudes toward men and mating.

Ten Stumbling Blocks to Marriage

In our work with women who want to get married but find it impossible to achieve, there are some themes that emerge over and over again as factors contributing to the fear of love. They might be called the Ten Stumbling Blocks to Marriage. You need to examine these issues in order to learn where to begin working with your fears. Consider each issue and ask yourself if it applies to you.

1. Beliefs You may not believe that there is a man who would love you, or that you even deserve being loved. Your profound fear of rejection may cause you to be very self-protective when you relate to men. You need to work on believing in your self-worth and your human entitlement to be loved.

2. Relationship Trauma Past heartbreaks create aloofness and a deep fear of emotional bonding. You may be unaware that past relationships are still affecting you and causing unconscious fear. Have you ever been deeply hurt? You must work through your grief over past relationships and recognize your need to be loved.

3. Success Syndrome You may have channeled your love needs into the professional arena and have tried to make career success substitute for love. If so, you must learn how to love a man and how to relinquish your perfectionism in the search for a marriage partner. Excessive perfectionism (no one's good enough) can mask emotional insecurity in a woman who is successful in work but unfulfilled in love. Being too demanding doesn't work well in a relationship.

4. Singles Scene Participating in the adult dating scene has little to do with courtship leading to marriage. Keeping your social life on this superficial level masks your fear of getting serious and taking responsibility. You need to admit how much you want a traditional marriage and not be afraid to assert yourself in order to make marriage possible.

5. Lack of Permission It's not unusual for a single

woman to discover in therapy that someone important in her childhood didn't give her permission to get married. This lack of permission can be conveyed through a mother's jealousy, a father's possessiveness, a prohibition on dating and numerous other indirect messages that are understood unconsciously to mean "Don't get married." If you lack permission to marry you'll be afraid of breaking the rules, and may feel ashamed of any man you are dating, as if he doesn't "measure up." You must learn to give yourself permission to be fulfilled in love.

6. A Disappointing Father Many a single woman describes her father as a disappointing individual. You may have lacked respect for your father, or you may have been hurt by his distance, his sarcasm or his physical cruelty. Whatever the specific circumstances, you might be unconsciously imprinted with an image of all men as potential disappointments. If men are not to be trusted, you'll actively protect yourself from them. You need to stop seeing your father's face on the men you are meeting.

7. Mother's Marriage A great many women today do not want to repeat the dynamics of their mothers' marriages. They are afraid of falling into servile patterns in which their own selfhood is diminished. Because of your mother's marriage you may not know how to assert a positive feminine perspective within marriage because you have no role models or support for being a self-respecting wife. By valuing and asserting your own needs you will not become a doormat in a relationship.

8. Value System There are single women who are discovering that marriage is extremely important to them, and regret that they haven't sought the partners who would bring them satisfaction. You may believe that you have made some wrong choices by not getting married earlier. Don't let regret hold you back. Appreciate the fact that we all operate out of blind spots, and that it is never too late to get in touch with what you want for the next phase of your life.

9. Lack of Cultural Support Courtship is a community ritual, and women today lack the mentors, role models and parental involvement that lend support and help usher them into marriage. You may be afraid of directing this area of your life yourself, but you probably also fear letting other people tell you what they think would be good for you. Like all of us, you need support to give you courage in making vital life changes.

10. Fear of Domination It's natural to resist being dominated by another person, and everyone resists marriage on this basic level. Women today especially value their freedom and are terrified of making even small compromises. However, if you want to marry, you must understand how to maintain your sense of self within marriage, and also how marriage can support rather than diminish your development as an individual.

These are among the many reasons to justify your fear of getting close to a man and loving him. In going through this list, check those items that are particularly significant for you. Each check mark represents an inner barrier to seeking intimacy. It is important to admit your fear and to reach out for intimacy in spite of it. By carefully considering each of these issues, you may become aware that there are many barriers within yourself preventing you from connecting to the intimate relationship that you want and need.

·4·
RELATIONSHIP SABOTAGE

When a man who could be a potential partner comes into your life, he may try to get close to you—uncomfortably close. There is a feeling that the usual boundaries between you and other people are not quite in place with this person. He gets under your skin, to use a common metaphor. He observes you more closely than you are accustomed to, and he assumes a bit more familiarity than a stranger normally would. He may dare brief moments of intimacy by focusing on you. He might indicate a desire to spend time alone with you, or when you are in a group situation he might speak directly to you, showing awareness of your reactions. Small gestures let you know that this man is moving in your direction. How do you react to someone who is interested in you? Are you available for male attention?

Maybe you are saying to yourself, "Nobody is making advances toward me. I wish they were!" Most likely that is *not* the case. Nearly every single woman we have worked with has a man or several men in her life. But a typical single woman doesn't consider her loyal pal George, her friend Bill from school who just got divorced and nurses a secret crush on her or the cute guy in the building who says hello in the elevator to be "contenders." We suggest that you relax a bit and consider any and all men to be possible partners, and focus upon *your* reactions when a man makes a gesture of special friendliness toward you.

You must figure out if you are among the many single women who register automatic rejection whenever a man makes a move that shows interest. Your rejection may not be conscious, but it triggers behaviors that sabotage the relationship. Some women are so quick to reject a man that they aren't aware they just missed an opportunity. When you are so fearful and vigilant, you don't let the inner melting, expansive process occur that creates a set of positive signals for a man. Your behavior makes it difficult for him to approach you.

Let's now look analytically at your behavior when you are with a man, in order to understand what you might be doing that causes relationships to fail from the start. There are two basic sabotage styles: active and passive. Active sabotage consists of aggressive responses that are meant to scare a man away. In active sabotage you come on too strong when a more gentle response is appropriate to what has been offered. (Remember that he is making himself vulnerable when he shows interest.) The passive sabotage style is more subtle, but can be equally devastating. It consists of things you are not doing. In passive sabotage you refuse to reciprocate when a generous response is required to keep strokes flowing. It takes two to tango, and with passive sabotage you refuse to dance. It would be very tidy to be able to say that women who are extroverts tend to use active sabotage and introverts engage in passive sabotage, but that isn't always the case. Women who are normally very outgoing can become quite cold and distant when they want to protect themselves from a man's friendly advances.

Active Sabotage

A MASK OF SMALL TALK

Being intimate means taking the risk of being honest and sharing something of yourself that you value. Usually, the more people talk the closer they get. But you can also use small talk as a way to avoid closeness. When you talk too much about trivialities, it confuses a man who is looking for honest, self-revealing contact. Your empty chatter dilutes the communication between you so that nothing important is happening. If you are afraid of getting close, a quiet moment in the conversation can be unnerving. When he is inviting or attentive, you might feel uncomfortable about the feelings he stimulates in you. Therefore, you talk a lot to suppress those feelings and stay in emotional control. When you do all of the talking, you reduce a man to the role of audience. You may think you are being very entertaining and articulate, but the true message you communicate is: "Admire me, but keep your distance."

COMING ON TOO STRONG

The real problem with active sabotage maneuvers is that they render a man passive. When you come on too strong, you take the wind out of his sails by expressing more interest than he does. If he is genuinely reaching out to you, his initial gestures are usually subtle, even tentative. You will scare him away with strong or demanding responses just as he is beginning to make himself vulnerable. When a man feels attracted to you, he is in a state of emotional arousal, and you want to keep him in this active mode, not reduce him to passivity by a barrage of energy. That's why it's important initially for your intentions to be somewhat of a mystery to him. He should question whether or not you are interested; no self-respecting man wants a woman who is going faster than he is. Staying on his wavelength is an experience in intimacy, and if you exercise restraint it will assure you of more intimacy in the future. There is truth in the cliché that a woman who is somewhat hard to get is appealing to a man. He must feel that the pursuit is his idea. Remember: Allure is subtle.

BEING SEXUALLY AGGRESSIVE

A man is delighted to be seduced, but that's not going to make him want to get you to the altar. The woman who obviously maneuvers a man into a hotel room or to her apartment is sending him unrewarding messages about the nature of their relationship. She isn't stimulating his desire to get to know her as a person, but is letting him put her in a quick, convenient category:

someone to sleep with when he feels horny. This is not to say that sex is not important: It's beneficial to creating a lasting relationship—but only after you have other powerful forces working for you. That means that you shouldn't satisfy a man's sexual desires easily. If you do decide to have sex with him, he should feel that it was his idea if you want him to remain in active pursuit of you. But if you really want to be close to a man, the best strategy is to let the relationship grow slowly so that when you do have sex it will be very meaningful and intimate.

MAKING HIM JUMP THROUGH HOOPS

When you are afraid of a man, you may need him to prove to you that he is trustworthy—over and over again. However, suspicious, fearful expectations hinder your ability to read intentions and judge character accurately. A fearful woman finds herself setting up little trials for a man and judging him on his performance as he jumps through the hoops she has erected. For a dinner date, maybe she firmly believes that the man should pick the restaurant and that if he asks her where she wants to go he is a wimp. Out of insecurity, do you set up a maze of meaningless tests a man must pass to win your approval? Excessive, petty demands do not make a man feel good about himself—nor about you. You operate on the underlying assumption that he is going to do something to disappoint you. Most self-respecting men give up on a woman who makes them jump through hoops.

Passive Sabotage
·

REMAINING ALOOF

Do you subject the men in your life to "Winter in Siberia"? If you are utterly cold with a man, he will think you don't like him even if secretly you are attracted to him. And yet, in spite of your aloof manner, you can be very lonely inside, wondering why he then doesn't pay more attention to you. Numerous men may feel attracted to you from a distance, but they don't approach you because your demeanor is so forbidding and standoffish. Being too serious is a form of passive sabotage because intimacy is essentially playful and tender. An attitude of sternness, which is your way of trying to conceal your loneliness, can make you appear to be haughty and judgmental. If your fears make you terribly self-conscious, you won't be tuned in to a man's overtures because you are so absorbed in yourself and worried about showing your vulnerability.

BEING NONRESPONSIVE

When a man shows some interest in you, the ball is in your court, and it's time for you to respond. If you are deeply insecure about being loved, you may not even register the fact that someone is showing interest. But many women simply don't acknowledge and affirm a man's gestures of interest even if they notice his attention, thinking they're playing a clever game of hard-to-get. If you are one of these women, you must realize you are playing it badly, because a good player offers some bait to keep a man interested. Men are insecure too, so their initial gestures are guarded. You can't wait to be chased, since that happens only in the movies. To avoid sabotage, you must be responsive and return a man's strokes so that he won't feel discouraged or rebuffed. If you consistently fail to pick up on your opportunities, eventually you won't have any.

BEING EASILY TURNED OFF

This form of passive sabotage occurs when a woman feels a small annoyance and then uses it to justify a negative overreaction. A woman who has been hurt in a relationship in the past has her defenses up and usually expects to be hurt again. Looking to blame someone, she is quick to be annoyed, insulted or turned off by some little thing that a man does or doesn't do. She expects problems, and pulls back fast when she spots trouble. Her withdrawal is such a strong automatic reflex that she herself may be unsure exactly what was off-putting. Even if she senses that she has misunderstood a man, or that he inadvertently triggered her vulnerability, she still holds *him* responsible for her negative reactions.

LETTING HIM GET AWAY

A woman who is experiencing her own fears of getting close finds herself in an impossible situation when she is dealing with a man who has his own deep fears. When he expresses any tentativeness, she is very quick to assume that his doubts are an ultimatum. She allows his ambivalence to tip the balance, and lets him back off. A woman who has never experienced getting what she wants from a man doesn't know that a simple argument or misunderstanding doesn't necessarily mean the end of things. She doesn't know that she can press infinitely farther than she does to work things out between them. A woman will often let a man escape because she doesn't know how to focus her feelings of upset into an effectively assertive stance that will help a man give her what she needs.

Sexual Sabotage

We are all too aware of the danger of casual sexual experimentation and recreational sex in this time of the AIDS crisis, but there is another important reason to avoid sexual intimacy early in a relationship. This is not a throwback to puritanism, nor does it suggest that there is something wrong with sex. But we are convinced that women today can have a major blind spot in not understanding how to harness sexual energy in the interest of forming a loving commitment. We have found from our clinical experience that when a woman patient fully understands *why* we advise her to withhold sex in the early stages of a relationship, it's much easier for her to make a relationship work in her best interest. The reasons for this have to do with our observations about the psychology of human courtship, as well as with the knowledge that men use sex to avoid becoming intimate and committed.

In most cultures in the past, sexual activity was not allowed until young members of the community went through certain rituals. Physical maturation indicated when they were physically ready to mate, but the culture guided people in the even more crucial step of knowing when they were psychologically ready to mate. The "old days," with their rules, rituals and chaperones, were not prohibitive of love, but rather structured things to make love more tantalizing, special—and possible. Through the stages of courtship rituals, which are usually very romantic, people learned how to love. "Unsophisticated" earlier generations knew something the swinging singles do not: If you have sex too soon, this romantic phase never gets fully developed.

You might think that having sex is a pleasant enhancement to the development of good feelings between two people. But sex without love, or before love has a chance to get started, makes it very difficult for two people to develop the depth of relationship that is needed for marriage. The best psychological model for courtship leading to marriage is a chaste friendship.

Women must realize that many men tend not to integrate love and sex in the way most women do, and that men will easily disconnect from their loving feelings when they feel vulnerable. In the early stages of a relationship a man might press for sex as an avoidance of getting emotionally involved, actually using sex as a defense against real closeness. When you exercise your power to withhold sex, you allow a man to get in touch with his deeper needs for you as a whole person rather than merely as a sex object.

One of the reasons you are tempted to have sex before

you are ready for love is because you and your partner feel anxiety. Caught in the push-pull between attraction and resistance, you look to sex as the magic answer to getting together in spite of the differences that make you both uncomfortable. However, sex will not resolve your ambivalent feelings. It may even fixate your relationship at an undeveloped level and you'll become aware that you are not going anywhere together despite the seeming closeness of sex. Instead, you need to work through any issues that are bothering you, letting yourself feel all of those uncomfortable and contradictory feelings that people feel when they are getting to know each other.

A lot of energy is needed for mating, and the buildup of positive aggression shouldn't be dissipated sexually. Don't worry about the frustration; it can lead you both to work harder at resolving important issues, fighting through the barriers that keep you from being closer. Sex too early in the mating game drains off all the natural energy needed to form what biologists call a pair-bond. In courting you must learn how to be romantically crazy about each other and to enjoy the prospect of planning your future together.

If you want to have recreational sex with someone, you must keep in mind that it may not lead to marriage. If you want to form a deeper relationship, let a special, romantic friendship develop without having sex. There is an old-fashioned principle that a woman is foolish not to acknowledge: Sexually she has something that the man desperately wants. Why should she give it to him easily? Sex is really special and should be the most tender, moving, joyful experience on earth. Treat it as sacred. When you have a powerful sexual encounter in the context of a deep love bond, it is an experience you will never forget. It's a shame to have sex just because you're anxious about getting close. When you feel yourself getting nervous, *stay nervous*. It will get you in touch emotionally.

When you take things too fast, it's very hard to go back and start over. Sex gives a partner too much access to your whole life, revealing a spectrum of personal stuff that is better to know in the context of love. Books and magazine articles advising you in the art of man-pleasing can lead you astray. The art of seduction, lovemaking, feeding him his favorite meal—none of these will distinguish or enhance your relationship. The carnal approach to things is not the hook that engages a man. A man will become most attached to the woman who inspires his loving feelings.

Sabotage Attitudes

You may be harboring some sabotage attitudes that you must change if you want to get married. For example, the best way to get someone to like you is for you to genuinely like him. Ask yourself honestly about your *generosity* in dealing with a man. He will be quick to pick up on your unconscious attitudes anyway, and if you are critical, he'll feel it, wishing that you be tolerant. If you are withholding, he certainly would prefer that you be friendly. If you are self-consciously wrapped up in yourself, it would be much better if you were tuned into him. He would prefer you to take his serious thoughts seriously instead of discounting them with superficial responses. A man also needs a woman to be generous enough to not expect too much of him. He might not know how to help heal your wounds from the past, even if he would like to. The sabotage attitude is *ungenerous*. You must learn how to give a man a break and accept him with his normal, human limitations. With a spirit of generosity, you will gain perspective about which problems are serious drawbacks to a committed relationship and which are minor shortcomings.

When you do things to sabotage a relationship, you are showing symptoms of your underlying fear of love. Sabotage keeps you from connecting with a man when you have a chance at love. Examine your behaviors, and be honest about whether you might be your own worst enemy when it comes to finding the marriage partner you claim to be looking for.

1. Be in touch with the fact that you need and want love.

2. Be in touch with your feelings of discomfort when a man wants to get close to you, and learn slowly to tolerate and be comfortable with the closeness that you desire.

3. Catch yourself when you are registering automatic rejection, and give yourself a chance to get to know a man.

4. Don't hide behind a mask of small talk, thereby trivializing yourself and the relationship. Share who you really are, and let him share himself with you.

5. Don't come on stronger than a man and take away his initiative in getting to know you.

6. Don't make a man prove himself on the basis of

silly tests that you devise for him based on your own insecurities.

7. Don't be cold and aloof, but approach men in a friendly manner, as fellow human beings.

8. Acknowledge and affirm a man's gestures of friendliness toward you.

9. Recognize if you are quick to get insulted or turned off, and learn to give a man a chance in spite of your insecurities.

10. Don't be quick to let a man get away because he has his moments of doubt. Hang in there and do your utmost to work things out.

11. Don't be sexually aggressive or let a man sexualize your relationship in order to avoid really getting close to you.

12. Let a man get to know you as a person, so that he has a chance of becoming romantically inspired.

13. Be generous, reminding and reassuring a man by your attitudes and behaviors that you really do like him.

14. Don't panic when there are minor problems. Try to solve them. When you can't, enjoy each other anyway.

·5·
LIVING FOR YOURSELF ALONE

This is the age of the career woman. Women's gains in achieving access to male-dominated professions are a hallmark of our times. Feminists complain that in corporate life there are but a few token women at the top of the corporate ladder, and usually only at the bottom of the top. Nevertheless, the sheer numbers of women in the work force are a dramatic increase from even ten years ago. We are in the middle of a career revolution for women.

When Career Comes First

If you are a career woman, you are a pioneer. You have uprooted yourself from home and hearth and have traveled into the world of work outside the home. There were no maps and few guides for you, and you have

probably experienced painful encounters with male resistance to your advancement on the job. You have
learned to keep going in spite of how bruised you feel,
and you have developed a serious, committed approach
to achieving your career goals. The price, however, has
been high. You have probably abandoned the inner
world of romantic thinking in which women focused
upon their desires for intimate contact with a mate.
Instead, you have prepared your mind for the assault
on the corporate ladder.

Victoria, thirty-eight, is a lawyer. She is single, and
works against the odds in her firm that offer no prec-
edent for female advancement. She has reached the
bottom of the top. It has become not good enough; she
presses for higher status. All her energy goes into learning political strategies at work—"remedial" lessons for
a woman who grew up learning the female art of people-
pleasing. She struggles to curb her tendency to give
more than is asked for and to ask for very little in return.
It has been difficult for Victoria to develop aggressive
self-interest, and even harder to spot it in her colleagues
when they are manipulating her. She knows that a competitive frame of mind must be learned in order to survive, let alone to advance to a higher position.

Victoria came to therapy wondering why she was still
single. "Do I intimidate men?" she asked herself. Perhaps she does intimidate men who have never known
professional women, but that is not really her main problem. It became clear that she had not put her energy
into learning relationship skills, nor had she stayed in
touch with herself emotionally. Through the years she
has fought her inclination to be generous and has be-

come enmeshed in self-interest. She has learned to think rather than to feel, making emotions the enemy of accomplishment. To Victoria, being "professional" means putting work before feelings. Like an athlete in training, she has turned away from her immediate emotional desires in a single-minded pursuit of career goals. Her life's objective is to rise in her firm, not to find emotional fulfillment.

RELINQUISHING INTIMACY

The mental attitude that creates autonomous behavior and success in the workplace is the opposite of the concern for connectedness and attachment that creates solid marriages. In creating an autonomous, self-reliant way of life, many women have sacrificed the ability to connect intimately with a mate.

Stress specialists cite the opposing roles of nurturer and worker as being difficult for one woman to perform. If a married woman tries to do it all—to have a career and also nurture a husband and children—she usually falls short in the role of traditional housewife. A single woman, whose focus is upon self-sufficient functioning, simply doesn't have the experiences that allow the nurturing and connecting aspects of her personality to develop.

OVERLY CRITICAL ATTITUDES

The autonomous, career-minded woman is often excessively critical of men, and has impossibly high standards. She is busy giving birth to herself. Struggling to overcome her own weaknesses, she is intolerant of any perceived weakness in others. Zealously developing herself, she is impatient with the petty hassles that relationships bring. She would rather be preparing for the next sales conference than explaining to her boy-friend that she didn't mean to make him angry the day before. Focused upon the obstacles at work that most women face, her energy will be aggressive and task-oriented, not connected to the spirit of nurturing or whimsy that magnetizes the love needs of a man.

Are you too compulsive to be sensuous? Too preoc-cupied to be inviting? Too hurried to notice the subtle gesture that denotes a real opportunity for intimacy? Busy making yourself invulnerable, you will lose the chance to explore the dynamic power your vulnerability has to inspire passionate, protective feelings in a man. In fact, male protectiveness may feel insulting if you take fierce pride in your self-sufficiency.

SUBLIMATING EMOTIONS

The three qualities necessary for intimacy are *openness*, *empathy* and *warmth*. But if you are bent on career suc-cess you learn to sublimate your emotions in the interest of the task at hand and the team you work with. You learn to make the tough decisions in spite of what you feel or how you care. You stop smiling, because you have learned that warmth dilutes your power and your credibility. The corporate mentality teaches you that kindness equals weakness, and that looking too happy can make you appear less than intelligent.

When you become closed, heartless and cold, you

can play the corporate game of power and success with the best of them. Then you learn to cover your ruthlessness with a veneer of charm, with a manipulative pseudo-warmth that looks and sounds inviting but gives nothing personally. If, as is likely, you begin to apply the same tactics in your love life, your lack of genuine warmth will put off a man who is seriously looking for love.

Without openness, you have no ability to disarm a man, and without empathy he will never discover why he needs you. In short, the very meaning of being "professional" leads to your unavailability for love. The single career woman who truly wants to marry must ask herself, "Do I still have a chance to learn how to entwine my life with someone else's?"

THE PRICE OF INDEPENDENCE

At a certain point in their lives, many autonomous women begin to mourn the loss of the married life that might have been. Pioneers do get homesick, and women long for men to reawaken the mating consciousness they relinquished when they became so career-centered. The first stirrings of longing for a man are often indications of a larger desire growing within you for a life oriented around human connectedness. Women get tired of trailblazing and want to go home, but the homes they yearn for never got built, because homes are usually created within the context of wanting to please a man and nurture his children. Many career women never imagined they would want such "old-fashioned" things and so never made them a goal in their lives.

In childhood you may have sensed your mother's struggle to have some life of her own, and you may have determined not to lose yourself as she did in the role of "just a housewife." But you may not fully appreciate (nor perhaps did your mother) the elaborate and satisfying system of family with mother as the hub of the wheel. Times are changing, and you may feel this loss more than the gains of your independent life.

Staying in Your Own World

The desire to avoid a submissive status in relationship to men can lead you into a loveless life. Women have come to feel that they must choose between marriage and selfhood. In a recent televised interview, Gloria Steinem cited the alarming statistics (now proven erroneous) that women over forty had only a twenty-two percent chance of getting married. She posed the question as to whom we should feel sorry for, the twenty-two percent who marry or the seventy-eight percent who stay single. Are the lucky ones perhaps the single women who have more of a chance of belonging to themselves?

Many independent women are now reconsidering marriage, but find themselves enmeshed in a lifestyle that has no place for a man. A positive sense of self is an important goal, yet self-orientation in the extreme leaves little or no room for another person in your life. When a woman is putting all of her energy into herself and her work, she gets out of touch with the ways men and women make contact. Operating in the realm of selfhood, she is concerned only with the details of her own life. They form a preoccupation—and, at worst, an obsession—so that she completely misses opportunities for contact or for mating. Those qualities we used to attribute to spinsterish schoolteachers or librarians—obsessiveness about details, an out-of-touch way of relating, off-putting mannerisms—can develop in any of us if we organize everything around ourselves and have little experience with socializing and intimacy.

This chronically preoccupied mood is illustrated in the following scene. Imagine that you are standing on a street corner. A stranger approaches and asks you for directions to a nearby museum. Absorbed with your own agenda, you are annoyed and you show it, or you just tune him out. Perhaps you should forget your train of thought for the moment and have a real person-to-person exchange with this stranger. Insular, single women have a tendency to remain in their own worlds, and not pick up on opportunities for contact.

Self-Absorption Can Block True Love

The marketplace capitalizes on our unconscious hunger for love and mating in advertising everything from liquor and cigarettes to jeans and underwear. The true psychological appeal of these advertisements, however, is more to our narcissism than to a love that reaches outward. Excessive self-involvement is a barrier to the kind of love that people need. Narcissists, for all their richly cultivated charm, are among the loneliest people around.

A close cousin to narcissism is materialism. Possessions can become substitutes for people, tangible security blankets that are held dear in the absence of deep love bonds. By clinging to yourself or to your worldly goods, you leave no space for a beloved partner to enter your life and touch you deeply. Maybe that's one reason why loving seems so much easier for the young—with few worldly goods and limited self-awareness, they can freely give to each other, spontaneously reaching out for the love they need. They have not learned to substitute self-indulgence for loving contact.

Margo was a member of a therapy group we conducted. She made her grand entrance every Tuesday night—usually late—and we all found ourselves quietly stunned by her appearance. She often wrapped herself in a silver fox coat, doused herself in expensive perfume and secured her beautiful blond hair with glittering combs. Margo owned a company, a specialty line of cosmetics sold through beauty salons. Her jet-set lifestyle sounded so impressive that it eclipsed whatever anyone else had to talk about. Margo's contributions to the group fell into one of two categories: bragging and complaining. Nobody could really make contact with her. When she bragged she didn't seem to notice the admiration she inspired. And when she complained, she described all the people in her life as if they were conspiring to give her a hard time. Everyone in the group backed off, afraid of being one of the objects of her anger and disappointment. Occasionally Margo cried desperately, sharing her loneliness, but her despair was hard to believe since she came across as a woman who had so much more than everyone else.

Eventually, the group became bored with Margo, and even ceased to admire her obvious assets; she now suffered the neglect that befalls every narcissistic person. And as the other group members withdrew from her, Margo became more self-indulgent, dramatically relating her latest accomplishments. She didn't notice how she had distanced the others, but we suspected that she felt their withdrawal on some level. It became a vicious circle: The more other people moved away, the more she clung to herself, which drove them farther away still. Soon she spoke with superiority about how she didn't need the group anymore.

We told Margo that we had an idea that might make a positive difference in her life, but that she had to be willing to try it for the following six sessions. She was intrigued. "You are not to mention anything about yourself for the next six weeks," we told her. "Instead, listen carefully to what other people are saying. Tune into them, and figure out what you might offer that would be helpful. Just listen to others, and care about them." She was shocked. "Isn't therapy the one place where it's okay to talk about yourself?" she protested. Firmly, we asked her to trust us enough to follow our suggestion because she might learn something important.

During the first session Margo was quiet, pouting like an unhappy child. The next session challenged her a little. Her pride had emerged and she wanted to prove that she could be a good listener. As she awkwardly offered others some bits of advice, she seemed to become more vulnerable. We began to see the part of Margo that was uncertain of her worth. By the third session she was no longer hiding behind the mask of "being impressive." She was beginning to really listen to others. As this process continued, group members showed some real affection for Margo.

During the following sessions she discovered that the real way to draw people to her was by forgetting herself and caring about them. Later, she thanked us all for helping her to give up her desperate self-aggrandizement. She told us how much it meant that she was learning to tune into others. For the first time in her life she was receiving strokes for being a real friend and it gave her a deep sense of self-worth.

Our materialistic culture celebrates the narcissistic woman. We see her image on the covers of countless magazines. She enters our homes on television. What you may not realize is that this is the image of the lonely woman. She is alone with her clothes, her cosmetics, her rituals. The only one speaking to her is her mirror, which—like most mirrors—probably speaks more of her flaws than of her beauty. This is not to suggest that a certain amount of self-care is not important, but narcissistic self-absorption definitely creates the wrong kind of energy for loving contact. You draw people to you when you reach out to them. There are a lot of single women like Margo who need to be released from self-involvement in order to be free to give and receive love.

Reaching Out

A businessman described a woman he met on an airplane. "She was an attractive person, but she had no desire to be attractive to *me*. I talked to her, but there were no signals coming my way from her." Women in

the workplace have learned not to give out subtle mating signals to men, who previously related to them by
flirting. But now, many women who have turned those
switches off are wondering how to turn them on again.

The missing ingredient is a kind of charming warmth.
To claim self-respect and an authentic identity, career
women have abandoned "feminine wiles" and artifices,
wanting to be regarded as people first and females second. But in mating, the *differences* between the sexes
need to be highlighted, and charm plays an important
part in bringing men and women together.

Charm is grounded in exhibitionism, and it is human
to want to show off for the opposite sex. A woman and
a man who are making mating gestures to one another
are in touch with this primitive desire to expose themselves in a way that will attract the other. In doing so
they enjoy the process as well as the prospect of reaching
the treasured goal of intimacy. Mating gestures are often
extremely subtle, even unconscious, but the mind is
rapidly and continually checking out the other person
and responding. The fact is, if you want to mate, you
must appeal to a man's desire to be charmed by you
and to his urge to impress you.

When a woman asks, "Will I ever find Mr. Right?"
we ask her: "Would you know what to do if you did
meet him?" Often the answer is no. In this age of career
emphasis, the female skills of shaping relationships have
become a lost art. Women are no longer giving relationships their best efforts. Many women do know some
available men (although they are reluctant to admit it).
Instead of asking yourself where all the men are, you
need to ask yourself how you can go about attracting

them. If your energy is focused upon single-minded achievements, you have learned how to be single, not how to be married.

There Is Hope: Making Marriage Possible

As we've shown, if you have worked hard to develop yourself as an individual in order to be successful in your career, you have stressed the opposite qualities of character from those needed in mating. Yet our aim was not to leave you feeling bitter or cheated. There is another, more hopeful point to be made: A developed, self-confident woman has special talents to offer in making relationships work—*once she puts her energies to that task*.

Today, many an enlightened man is looking for an equal partner, and prefers a strong woman. He wants a woman who can share the stress and responsibilities of making it in the world. The self-development of a woman can be a great enhancement to marriage once she learns how to find the balance within herself between the nurturing and aggressive aspects of her personality. This is women's next psychological frontier.

But first things first: You must *make a place* in your life for the relationship you long for. By doing some of the following exercises, and making some important changes in yourself, you can begin to make yourself available for a committed relationship.

1. Begin to notice men—all kinds and all ages. Find what is attractive to you in looks and personality. There

is something special in almost everyone, and positive, warm perceptions of men in general are an important foundation for mating.

2. Make a list of ten men that you like, and make notes about what it is you like in them.

3. Think about the married people you know, and analyze one or two relationships that you admire. Imagine what the partners do together, and picture the time they spend with one another. Try to picture yourself involved in similar activities with someone.

4. Work on learning a cooperative mode of operating, moving beyond strictly autonomous, competitive behaviors. At work you could share a project; in private time serve on a committee, or reach out to someone in need. Like many career women, you may have lost perspective about communal activities.

5. Become a better listener. Let yourself relax when you're with others and forget about how you're coming across. Instead, give your attention to them; tune in and enjoy learning about them. Listen without judging or giving advice. This will teach you about the *process* of relating, which is very different from your job where the emphasis is on a work *product*. Achievements in relationships have to do with tuning in to another person. This takes a lot of practice.

6. Examine your own motivations for being self-sufficient. Are you making up for your mother's dependency? If so, reexamine this decision. Is loneliness too high a price to pay?

7. Be honest about your tendency to be overly self-absorbed. Without a genuine appreciation and interest in others, friends will find you to be one-dimensional

and empty, in spite of your impressive accomplishments. This is because there is nothing in the relationship for *them*.

8. Learn to flirt! Essentially this means revealing the part of you that is fun-loving, witty and cute. There is a playful kid inside everyone, and flirting is a kind of play between the sexes.

9. Dedicate the same energy to mating as you do to your work. That is what it takes. If you are unwilling to focus on this part of your life in order to make things happen, you'll know that healing your loneliness is not an important priority in your life. Most women who complain about loneliness do little or nothing about it. Once you decide to stop leaving things up to chance (do you leave your career advancement up to chance?) you will forcefully direct your energies toward finding a man and marrying him.

10. If you don't have a serious relationship, do one thing each week that will give you new exposure to men. Take a trip or go to a lecture, workshop, church group or party. Join a dating service, put an ad in the personals, answer an ad yourself. This way you'll be programming yourself to find someone, as well as making it possible.

·6·
THE FEAR OF
MARRIAGE

The current dilemma of single women has its roots in the work of such feminist writers as Simone de Beauvoir and Betty Friedan, who described the pain of women whose lives precluded developing their talents, asserting worldly power or exercising self-direction. Twenty years ago, when you were figuring out how to live your life, the passive, submissive, duty-bound woman's story was being told. The feminists warned that loss of self was too high a price to pay for the security and social acceptability of being married.

When women became free to admit that they were unhappily married or otherwise suffering from male domination, today's working woman was born. Having privately stopped believing in happily-ever-after, they soon discovered that their private pain was shared by their sisters. Women began to work consciously to transcend their psychological programming of duty (to men and children) before self. They began resisting marriage. You have been deeply influenced by feminism, by the voices that spoke of the futility of being a nurturing, housecleaning machine, and of the pain that results from the repression of your selfhood. In response, you rejected your mother's way of life. Instantly you lost a positive role model.

Not being like their mothers is almost an obsession for many single women who observed the diminished human spirit in their mothers as they struggled to be happy as housekeepers but felt mentally dulled and diminished by monotonous routines.

Don't underestimate the power of rejecting your mother's life in keeping you single. To you, being a wife, on some level, always means being "just a housewife," even today when you yearn for marriage. What a contrast you must have observed between your housewife mother and a female college professor, or later between your mother and a female supervisor at work. As the daughter of a traditional housewife, you developed a mixture of pity and contempt for the woman you never wanted to become. When you were young and energetic, you had large dreams that required an expansive future to explore your possibilities. Your mother's life seemed, by contrast, to be claustrophobic.

Can a Married Woman Belong to Herself?

When we got married and moved to Cleveland for the sake of Steve's job, Susan desperately missed her family, her community, her college years and her friends. No matter how loving Steve was, she felt captive, plunged into the culture of marriage, violently snatched from the pursuit of her selfhood and the people who had supported it. Susan had distinguished herself in college, but it was Steve who was going on to pursue academic life, and Susan was expected to support him by getting a job.

The future was a painful blur. She felt traumatized by her change of name, her change of religious tradition in marrying in Steve's church rather than her own, by her loss of any personal purpose. Once engaged, she never seriously asked herself what she wanted to do with her life. Steve seemed to love her talents and her values, but his love felt proprietary. Because she was appealing to him, he was happy to annex her life onto his own. Susan was ambivalent about being so loved by him. With little understanding of the nurturing her mind and spirit needed, Steve assumed that grafting her onto him would give her a life.

In retrospect, we know that there was too much of his turf, his assumptions and his ambitions in the mix, and not nearly enough of hers. Steve was very happy with their life, and wondered what was the matter with his wife emotionally. Why was she crying, even grieving, when everything was perfect for him?

The expectation of a symbiosis based on woman's selflessness and man's self-assertion leads a woman to relinquish something so basic, that it is almost impossible for her to understand that *her very self is missing.* Feminists have documented this painful loss of self within the traditional marriage system.

When you are with a man you will face some of the

same expectations that your mother faced, and you may be single today because you are unwilling to struggle with the inevitable entrapping aspects of married life. It is quite threatening for men to consider the idea that there are many women who simply do not enjoy home-making or nurturing activities. The archetypal image of the happy housewife exists because of everyone's wish to be mothered. This pressures women into unequal relationships in which the ego of only one person, the male, is served. Married women can still experience the same helplessness and hopelessness of peasant women of centuries ago. Married women still aren't allowed to have lives of their own, and must still fight for the right to have thoughts or interests that don't enhance their husbands or families. Women in all stations of life, married or unmarried, still often experience marriage psychologically as enslavement. We cannot underestimate the importance of work outside the realm of housework to keep a woman feeling like a person.

In order even to entertain the prospect of giving up your autonomy for marriage, you must be able to envision a life in which you maintain your autonomy *within* the demands of the relationship. You will be entering a struggle that you have entirely avoided by remaining single.

Giving Away Your Power

Many women we see in therapy who want to get married have been married before. They remember working through an after-the-honeymoon depression, and with idealistic energy spending a year or two trying to make a bad marriage work out.

Janet was married when she was twenty-one and divorced at twenty-six. Today at thirty-two, she speaks of her adult life as if it began at twenty-six. Her marriage memories are of a shadowy and bleak time when she tried hard to keep herself and the relationship going against impossible odds. Her husband complained constantly about her inadequacies as a wife. Those years look pitiful as she remembers a closed life with no possibilities, and her own demolished self-esteem. Life began with divorce and a new career in film production.

In discussing her loneliness today and her desire for a committed relationship, Janet blurted out what many women feel: "I can't conceive of being able to keep the strides I have made in my life if I marry and have a family."

Janet believes that marrying today would be a step back to her life at twenty-two. Sadly, her belief might prove correct. As competent as she is in her work, when she becomes involved with a man she becomes a diminished person. Within the context of a male-female love relationship she is so compliant and submissive that she allows a man to be utterly unaccountable to her.

Janet's problem begins when she is attracted to a man and finds herself falling for him. She wants the relationship to become closer and deeper, but at some point the man begins to distance himself from her. Her reaction is to act weak and stupid, refusing to engage him concerning his failure. Instead, she accepts his behavior and suffers.

In her professional life Janet is successful and skillful, even downright dynamic. Imposing her high standards on others, she has no trouble confronting an employee whose performance is not up to snuff. But with a man

who is disappointing her, Janet becomes deeply insecure and paralyzed in her ability to think clearly for
herself. Caught in a veil of mystification, she cannot
bring her realness and her basic identity to bear on the
situation. Instead of living in reality and demanding
accountability, Janet enacts a submissive charade.

In the presence of a man, this highly actualized woman
responds out of the cultural conditioning of women from
previous generations. She is unconscious of what is happening in her romantic life, looking and sounding positively stupid to the people who know her to be a self-
confident and strong woman in other situations. In this
compliant state, she puts up with mistreatment and
dares not open her mouth. We think that the reason
relates to profound lessons Janet and women like her
learned from their mothers when they were children.

We learn by identification. As we grow up, in an
automatic, unconscious way we do what we see others
doing. If your mother tolerated an abusive marital relationship, she taught you to tolerate one. The conditioning to be a submissive female is profound. You learned
how to relate to a man from a primitive and indiscrim-
inate identification with the woman you observed since
early childhood. You may be remaining single today
because you have not learned how to be self-respecting
in relation to men.

Whether or not you admired your parents' relationship, there will be an automatic compulsion to behave
in the way you learned as a small child. You automatically absorbed your mother's state of mind as she related to your father. That is why an otherwise dynamic
woman like Janet acts weak when she loves a man. She
is playing out her early programming and learning. In-

deed, she admitted in therapy that she saw her mother cry and passively complain about her father hundreds of times.

If you are inhibited in asserting your desire for accountability from a man, you won't be able to make the relationship work. If you are generally submissive around men, you probably believe that you can't maintain the independence and self-esteem you have achieved and still be married. In work, you'll operate on an autonomous basis, but in love you'll become a servant. At the very thought of confronting a man you freeze, as if the computer were given a task to do but doesn't have the right program to carry it out.

The Compulsive Nurturer

A variation on this theme involves the woman whose submissiveness expresses itself in another way: She is a compulsive nurturer. In the presence of men some women don't shut down; they go into high gear. These women don't suffer because men neglect them, but because when men are around they can't attend to themselves.

Jennifer told us that she cannot focus on herself if there is any other stimulus around. She gets overly concerned about the well-being of her boyfriend. She mends his clothes, helps him write his speeches, buys him clever presents. Because she is so active, she may not realize that she allows a man to dominate her very selfhood. She exerts a powerful and compelling presence in his life, but constantly feels herself losing ground in her own life. Jennifer manifests the classic problem that feminists have highlighted for us—the very presence of others makes "the other" the subject.

It's difficult to believe that a vivacious and generous woman like Jennifer feels empty inside. Relationships are draining to her because she gives too much and must retreat into solitude in order to feel like herself again. She must be alone in order to be the subject of her own life. Jennifer seesaws from the extremes of intense relationships to deep solitude.

Once you extricate yourself from drowning in the perceived neediness of others, you must be vigilant and work hard to cultivate healthy self-centeredness. Your intimates usually wonder what terrible thing has happened to you because you're not as "nice" as you used to be and you're saying no a lot more often to them. This is positive, but recovering compulsive nurturers must not handicap themselves by too much solitude, because that extreme breeds loneliness and stroke deprivation. If you're ever to get married, you must learn to have self-interest *within* the context of a relationship. Instead of reacting to the stimuli of others, you must be active in the pursuit of your independent wants and needs.

Because you learned from your mother to give up your power to husband and family and to compulsively nurture them at your own expense, you will understandably fear marriage. Often this fear is unconscious, just as your self-denial is automatic and unconscious. But on exploration it will become clear that you are avoiding marriage because you are afraid of it engulfing you. And why shouldn't you be afraid? Most people would want to avoid being that involved in weakness or servitude.

You must develop ways to keep your power, belong to yourself, and maintain an equal give-and-take with a man in order to become less fearful and more naturally disposed toward marriage. You must understand the ways you have been programmed to be an adaptable, people-pleasing female and learn new ways of relating to a man. Otherwise, you will equate marriage with inevitable and painful submission.

Here are the things you need to work on in making marriage seem like a worthy emotional goal:

1. Examine the relationship between your mother and father. Remember that it still profoundly influences your perceptions of marriage. On paper, write out the scene of a play in which your mother and father are the characters. Invent the dialogue between them, focusing on the dynamic that you found to be most unpleasant.

2. Look at the most serious relationship you ever had with a man. Write a similar dialogue, this time focusing on a conflict that the two of you had.

3. Analyze the role of the female in each of these dialogues. Look especially for underlying emotions of fear in the woman, and a desire to please the man at all costs.

4. Question your tendencies to make adjustments to men at your own expense. Are you afraid of not making a man happy? Are you afraid to object to his point of view? Are you afraid he will go away if you don't obsessively nurture him? Do you find it difficult to tell a man your side of things?

5. If you have serious problems with losing your sense of yourself in the presence of a man (many women do),

take an assertiveness training course in which you focus on this issue, or have a few Gestalt therapy sessions in which behaviorally you learn to play a more self-respecting role with men. Only when you change your learned behavior will you lose the fear of repeating your mother's marriage.

6. Desensitize yourself to the fear of male disapproval by practicing objecting to the opinions of men you know. Find the shade of difference in your own opinion—and express it! Men have to get used to the idea that it is not a woman's function in life to be an undiscriminating source of support to them. Get comfortable with telling the truth about your feelings and opinions in matters of little importance in the beginning, and build up courage for expressing it on matters of importance.

7. Promise that you will never lose yourself in a relationship, that your self-respect will never be sacrificed. A big issue for a woman in a marriage is knowing how to be on her own side when the husband she cares about has a different opinion. You must learn to give up supporting the man when he is clearly opposing your healthy self-development, and express your own truth.

8. Fantasize being married. Don't focus on the man, but on the way *you* operate. Picture yourself married and maintaining your friendships, your freedom to make decisions, your work, hobbies, other interests and your own point of view.

9. Observe women who are self-respecting individuals within their marriages. Replace your old image of the patriarchal marriage in which the man has the last word with a new relationship between equal partners.

·7·
THE POWER OF PAST HURTS

Every woman has a unique story to tell about her past experiences in intimate relationships. Reconstruct your memories of love and be aware of your own story, because it created a pattern for your future relationships. Even if some of those experiences were unhappy ones, you will unconsciously expect them to happen again.

If a recurrent pattern emerges as you recollect your past, you may be entrapped by it. But, you say, shouldn't I know better than to repeat painful experiences? We are not implying that you're a robot who blindly repeats herself, yet a love relationship has a special way of imprinting your mind and heart. Look beyond the pain of a past love and try to understand the deep attachment that was involved. Emotionally, and often unconsciously, you cling fiercely to people you have loved deeply, no matter what their faults. You must understand your love style in terms of those former intense attachments. Childhood relationships are especially significant. Your parents, who today may have marginal influence in your life, shaped your attitudes toward love profoundly.

An exciting part of our work is seeing that people can come to terms with the past and move on. Sometimes the mere recognition of a pattern breaks the curse of unhappy repetition. The following sections are guides to examining childhood love experiences. Use them to make your own connections to your present relationship patterns.

The First Person You Ever Loved

A woman's first love experience is with her mother. The intensity of that love is based on tremendous dependency and need, and an infant feels a primitive, urgent desire to attach herself to her mother. Here are the roots of the physical urge to press your body next to someone for comfort and nurturing, and the root of the desire to intertwine all the activities of your life with another person for support, recognition and appreciation.

A baby has the capacity to bond herself to her mother, grasping fingers and breasts, clinging to her clothing, pulling her hair. She gazes into her mother's face as she feeds with an intensely fixed stare, as if locking her mother's image permanently in place. Attachment is a baby's way of life; her cries are designed to keep Mother close, and her adorable communications invite Mother's loving attention.

Look at your relationship to your mother and try to imagine what it was like when you were young. Was she constant and reliable? Available for physical closeness? Was she intimate and playful and emotionally at ease with motherhood? If she was, then you too may be at ease and open to intimacy. If she was not available in this trusted way, you have probably developed hidden fears about getting close to others.

Here are some examples of limitations in a mother's love that result in resistance to intimacy.

A COMPETITIVE MOTHER

Melanie's mother imitated her interests, virtually stealing them from her, as well as her friendships with women and men. A few stabs at independent accomplishment triggered her mother's depression, anger or blatant disinterest. Today, Melanie continues to believe there is something wrong with herself. This is the destructive legacy of a jealously competitive mother.

A NEEDY MOTHER

Emily's mother was orphaned at two. When she gave birth to Emily, she unconsciously wanted her child to be the mother she never had. Emily, in turn, was deprived of the devoted mother she needed. "I used to think I was sad because my mother was so depressed," she said. "But this deep emptiness is really about the mother I never had." Emily had a minimal sense of her own unique self and didn't know how to be receptive to life's experiences. Being needy yet unreceptive is the common emotional problem of a woman whose mother was herself looking for a mother.

A POSSESSIVE MOTHER

There can be intimacy problems for daughters who are burdened with living in compensation for their mothers' unfulfilled potentialities. In high school Vicky received the lead part in the senior class play, but she determined not to tell her overly possessive mother. When her mother discovered the news, Vicky lost all her desire to participate in the play. Her accomplishments were being used to feed her mother's voracious appetite for vicariously living Vicky's life in order to get a sense of her own self. Vicky became a loner who equates love with intrusion and possessiveness.

AN ABUSIVE MOTHER

Most heartbreaking of all are the cases where mothers inflicted so much psychological damage that their daughters cannot deeply trust anyone. These women come to us utterly blocked in their ability to feel love. But still they cling to a shred of hope that their mothers were not at fault. "If my mother beat me, it must have been because I was a bad girl."

Jamie's mother sent her to boarding school when she was nine, and rarely visited her. Jamie became completely self-sufficient to protect her inner anger and hurt.

Estelle's mother left her daughter's rearing to the household servants so that she could travel around the world. Estelle missed her mother desperately, and was subjected to abuse and neglect by inadequately supervised caretakers.

Rosemary was regularly awakened in the middle of the night by her disturbed mother, who demanded that she and her little sister get up and clean the house.

Jody was physically beaten by her mother on many occasions. She sometimes volunteered for a beating to protect her younger sister.

Kay's mother flew into seemingly unprovoked rages, berating her for being bad, slapping and shaking her.

Children of abuse complain of a general sense of being disconnected. Lack of basic trust makes it hard to engage in either meaningful work or comforting relationships. These women seem to float about, participating briefly in relationships with unavailable men, fearing real contact. In therapy their eyes are glazed. They reject much give-and-take with their therapists. Our most severe cases of disengagement have been women with abusive mothers.

MOTHER'S BEST GIRL

There are some single women who have never made a break from their families to create separate lives. Mothers can be so powerful that their daughters remain forever children, looking to their mothers as their main resource in life. Some mothers dominate their daughters with what appears to be irresistible goodness, and the daughters don't experience enough ambivalence toward them or enough self-confidence to want to leave home.

This pattern is particularly common in families where the mothers were abundantly devoted to their children.

Even in cases where the daughters do not live at home, they spend their weekends and all vacations with their families. Mating seems out of the question.

A mother who creates the illusion that all resources are to be found within herself or within the home she has created limits her daughter's discovery of new people and other vital experiences that will fulfill her. Her daughter may unduly fear betraying the special closeness she feels with her mother. Was *your* mother good at bonding but not so good at letting you go?

Your Heart Belongs to Daddy

Fathers are magic. Fifteen-year-old Hilary described to us her feelings for her father: "My father is a complete source of support. I need what he gives me. He is the person who really makes me feel good about myself. When he tells me that I'm beautiful, or that I did something well, I soak up what he says. I expect him to tell me those things; I really count on his admiration. Your own father is the strongest source of appreciation, the person you want to hear compliments from the most.

"In a certain way, a father is like a pal because of how he talks to you. You're closest to your mother because she is so much like you, but your dad is different and that makes it fun. If your dad says something to make you laugh, it totally fills you up with happiness. I guess my feeling is that he is someone who really cares about me in a powerful way."

We asked this young woman if she would feel just as strongly about her father if he were not so expressive of his love.

"Of course I would," Hilary replied. "No matter what he did I would feel completely devoted. Your own father is the main man in your life. You don't feel the same at all about boys because they're immature. And with other men, like teachers or friends' fathers, you'll be formal. But your own father is a personal, special man.

"It's like he sees everything. He's watched your mother care for you and has observed everything about you. Sometimes you sense that he watches his family grow with a kind of awe. You feel connected to this person who knows you so well. It's a special familiarity that's hard to express. There is this feeling of excitement when your father comes home that you never would feel with your mother. You just respect your father so very much."

A father's very presence is a tremendous source of confidence, strength and security. This inspires intense loving devotion, showing how much a daughter needs her father's magic. Even if your father did not support you with strong affection, your loving attachment to him can be quite strong. He was one of the people you most wanted to have love you. He was the man you knew intimately, and who knew you well.

When women choose particular men, it is often because they are deeply attracted to qualities reminding them of their fathers. They can forget this powerful attachment too readily, not realizing what is happening when intense feelings are evoked by a man who acts tough, remote, depressed, angry or flirtatious—just like Dad. Attraction to particular characteristics is often the unconscious recollection of an undiscriminating, complete adoration of your father during childhood. You "see" something in a man that inspires the special feeling you had about your father when you were young.

As with your mother, the relationship with your father occurs so early in your life it affects you on a deeply primitive level for good or for ill. Interaction with your father results either in trust or fear. It's highly detrimental to future mating if you fear your father.

Alexis would sit silently at the family dinner table, frozen in fear that her overworked, uptight father would blow up at everyone.

Connie waited anxiously for her father to issue sarcastic barbs of criticism to her and her sisters.

Evelyn endured her alcoholic father's fearsome personality transformations—from amiable conversationalist to angry bully.

All of these women felt frightened whenever they were with their fathers. Even today they are afraid of being personally dressed down by Dad. When those feared moments do occur, these women experience an aching despair beneath the quiet, timid exteriors they present to their fathers.

Many men intimidate their families. They often feel powerless in the outside world, and only at home find opportunities to express their masculine "entitlement" to dominate others. Some fathers are so wedded to power games at work that they can't resist playing them at home as well. They enjoy feeling dominant, yet don't respect those whom they are able to bully. They are trapped in a macho frame of reference that doesn't enable them to appreciate, or even perceive, the value of generous, humble or loving people. They equate kindness with weakness. They believe inspiring fear is the way to win, and the spoils of their victories are broken relationships, demolished egos, ruined family trust.

Patricia's father, a college professor, used his intellectual tools effectively against both her and her brother. His children were so fearful of feeling "stupid" that they could not write papers in school, becoming brilliant college dropouts, losers at the expense of their father's enormous ego.

Aileen's physician father was a pillar of the community, but a tyrant at home. Exhausted whenever he tried to relax, he was a human time bomb. Asking him to help with a homework assignment or fixing a Christmas tree stand provoked wild temper tantrums in this saintly father. "You always bother me! I can never get my own needs met! Nobody ever thinks of me!" Everyone in the family felt hopeless; they could never please him. Little wonder that his daughter feared getting close to any man.

Women who fear their fathers are blocked in expressing loving feelings openly. Most of them continue to love their fathers in their thoughts, and long for fatherly affection, but they don't learn how to translate their loving thoughts into actions. The fact that you can still feel some love for Dad in spite of his shortcomings promises healing, however.

ABUSIVE FATHERS

Most often when we hear of serious abuse it is associated with alcoholism. Alcoholic fathers are a special breed, distant from their children and rarely close to their wives, yet given to temper outbursts and active violence. Andrea lived in fear of her father's irrational outbursts, spending her time at home in hiding, being as quiet and withdrawn as possible in order to avoid his wrath. Together with her mother and sisters, she figured out how to live by steering clear of him. There were the nights when he didn't come home. Andrea would wake from a troubled sleep as her father barged in the door. There would be screaming at her mother. Andrea became extremely timid and shy, avoiding men all of her life.

Many fathers are married to their jobs instead of being involved with their wives and children. Workaholics can have temper problems similar to alcoholics, but most of their damage comes from neglecting their families emotionally. Often they are regularly involved with other women, and divorce is common in such families.

Among the worst are fathers who commit acts of violence or sexually abuse family members.

If you have experienced a troubled, nonsupportive relationship with your father of any variety, from mild teasing to outright attempts to kill you, it will powerfully affect the quality and degree of closeness you experience with men in the mating process. With all of the imperfect family-life dramas that you have witnessed, it's not surprising you have an abundance of fears that work against easy mating.

Nevertheless, even if you were a victim of an abusive father, you must believe there is nothing the matter with you as a person. Intimacy and love are learned in families. If you have not had these experiences, you cannot expect to be able to mate easily. Fortunately, love is something that can be learned at any age. Uncovering the hidden fears that prevent you from getting married allows you to work on them and overcome them.

The Impossible Dream

It was a shocking notion in Freud's time that a child of three or four possessed an intense wish to marry the parent of the opposite sex. Something in Sophocles' ancient play about King Oedipus marrying his own mother must have hit home, however, because it became an enduring classic. Today we have no trouble accepting these "Oedipal" feelings: Dad, your first male relative, is your first "husband." The bond between the two of you is established in infancy. Only later do you learn the painful fact that Mom is your father's preferred, lifetime woman, and that you will someday need to be separated from him and marry someone else. The Oedipal desire is the desire not to get divorced from Dad.

Your Oedipal relationship actually included three people: Dad, Mom and you. This is a necessary aspect of childhood to be lived through. Unpleasant? Yes. But not to be skipped. Loving Dad but not being able to marry him is a core issue in the emotional growth process from girlhood to womanhood. If you are stuck in one part of this developmental stage, you may not be able to move into the final phase—marrying another man. Here are the eight Oedipal stages girls must pass through for healthy growth to occur:

1. *A Special Relationship with Daddy*—When you are a little girl you need and expect to be adored by your father. Your mother should support this special attach-

ment, giving it her blessing rather than feeling competitive or jealous.

2. *The Oedipal Dream*—This is a fantasy of marrying your father, a romantic dream of two people mating. In the dream you wish Mom would shrink into the background or die—accidentally, of course.

3. *Frustration of the Dream*—You realize that you never will marry your father. Mother is very much alive and would be angry if she knew your feelings, so the dream is put on hold, waiting to present itself in the future.

4. *A Nurturing Relationship*—You develop a more balanced relationship with both parents. At age four you were not ready to be a wife anyway, so you spend the next several years learning how to be like Mom, still secretly hoping to unseat her.

5. *The Second Oedipal Dream*—This fantasy emerges from its dormant state when you are a young teenager. In a trancelike fantasy you sit close to Dad while he watches TV, calling him "darling" like Mom does, suggesting that he restyle his hair like a member of Duran Duran.

6. *Transference of Oedipal Feelings*—This development starts in your teens as you discover there is a big world out there with many possible people to love including girlfriends, teachers and guys with the right haircuts who are sending out all the right signals.

7. *Dreaming a New Dream*—You meet a man who is probably like Dad in some ways you don't even consciously notice. He is a wonderful stranger with whom you can freely express your dream of mating. Mother has no part in this dream, so there are no more triangles getting in your way.

8. *Getting Married*—Two people court each other with

the intention of bringing their dreams together. Your desire for marriage is a reflection of the early hopes for staying close to Dad forever, which was your original Oedipal dream.

Analyzing your actual development against this list of the ideal passage through the various Oedipal stages will isolate key issues and problems you were left with in learning how to love and mate.

Did you experience a special relationship with your father or another close male who accepted your loving feelings in infancy and later?

Did your mother give her wholehearted blessing to that relationship?

Did you develop your feminine identity through a good relationship with your mother and through friendships with other girls and women?

Were your Oedipal wishes appropriately thwarted, so that you knew your father preferred your mother as his wife?

Did you then transfer your love from family members to friends and boyfriends?

Did you keep the feelings and desire for marriage of the original Oedipal dream alive?

Have you moved from the "triangle mentality" in which you love a married man to finding an available man for yourself?

It's easy to see why many therapists understand adult mating behavior in terms of the Oedipal drama. Women who have affairs with married men and imagine that their wives are either shrews or nonexistent are displaying true Oedipal (triangular) behavior, living in a fantasy world that never brings them real fulfillment.

The woman who looks for fathering in a love relationship is trying to kindle the original romantic dream that never properly blossomed in childhood, when it would have been appropriate. If she consistently dates unavailable men she is not unlike the girl who is not yet ready to be a real wife herself. Or if she plays the field, she is like the angry teenager whose feeling of romantic betrayal makes her release herself willfully from the limited options for love within her family.

Closing the Intimacy Gap

Last year the National Institute for Mental Health (NIMH) issued the results of a long-term research project conducted on the issue of happiness in marriage. One of the most interesting findings had to do with intimacy in adult life: The survey found that the amount of intimacy one experiences in adult life will directly correlate with the amount of intimacy experienced with one's parents during childhood.

A man who felt close to his parents when he was growing up will most likely feel close to his wife as an adult. A woman who felt coldness and distance between herself and her mother or father will feel a similar sense of isolation as an adult. The intimacy gap that you may be experiencing presently has a great deal to do with the way you were cared for by your parents. You are a creature of unconscious learning, and you can tragically repeat the past unless you take strong, conscious steps to become aware of your past and present patterns and change things.

When you are a victim of the intimacy gap, you are in the position of not really knowing how to be close. Without those early lessons, you must learn to love as an adult. It feels risky, but it's worth it.

Because you didn't have enough love from your parents, you don't know how to reach out and be close to people who are willing to love you. You may feel painfully lonely, but you aren't comfortable receiving the love you need. It's very important that you be aware of the connection between past deprivations and present self-depriving behaviors. To see if you are presently living out a loveless script that was given to you in childhood, ask yourself the following questions.

1. Do you resist meeting available men even when you have a good opportunity?
2. Is it hard to really believe that people like you even when you have evidence that they do?
3. Do you feel sad when you see that someone is happy with a partner, telling yourself that such good fortune isn't for you?
4. Do you have fantasies about imaginary men but have trouble connecting with someone in reality?
5. Does it seem as if there is always something terribly wrong with the men you know?
6. When you go out on a date do you expect inevitable disappointments?

If you answered yes to these questions, you have loveless attitudes, and you engage in the kind of loveless thinking that can be a self-fulfilling prophecy. The fol-

lowing questions will highlight the sources of those attitudes.

1. Do you remember feeling a close emotional
   attachment to your mother and father?
2. Do you believe that your mother and father
   love you today?
3. Do you fear your mother's or father's critical
   attitude toward you?
4. Do you think you have disappointed your
   mother or father, or that what you do is never
   quite enough?
5. Do you resist telling your mother or father what
   is going on in your life, because the response
   is likely to spoil things for you?
6. Is your mother happy with the quality of love
   in her life?
7. Did your mother or father ever do anything to
   hurt you emotionally or physically?
8. Did you feel as you were growing up that your
   mother or father loved someone else much more
   than you?
9. Did you experience the loss of a parent through
   death, illness or divorce during your childhood?
10. Do your parents express loving emotions phys-
    ically and verbally?

Your answers to these questions will reveal the emotional legacy of your childhood. You may presently harbor expectations of abuse or neglect. You may believe
that when someone really gets to know you, they can't

possibly care for you. Such beliefs are learned, and have nothing to do with present reality—unless you continue the patterns of the past yourself. You must challenge the belief that there is no love for you, because believing you are lovable is what makes it true.

Take the risk of discovering that you no longer need to be victimized by the shortcomings of parents who loved you inadequately. The real learning is when you let yourself get close to other people and discover that everyone is lonely and needy of love. Everyone, to a greater or lesser degree, struggles with the fear of being rejected. By reaching out to one another, we can heal our loneliness. It takes courage, but none of us need to relive the unhappiness of the past.

·8·
DOOMED RELATIONSHIPS: WHEN WOMEN DENY THEIR FEARS

If you are deeply afraid of love you won't even know that you carefully seek situations in which you can cleverly avoid feeling your fear of getting close and possibly being hurt. You have within you a mechanism that shields you from painful emotional realities so you never need know they exist. It is known as denial. When denial is operating you won't know it because psychological defenses are unconscious. Denial is an anesthetic, protecting you from past emotional wounds and memories of troubled relationships.

In our experiences with women who complain about being single, we often see them turning to relationships that are doomed from the start. Fear leads them to look for "safe" relationships that are not safe at all. This chapter is about women who are unaware that they fear love and its possibly painful consequences and who protect themselves by hiding within impossible relationships.

Pretending to Love: Escape into Fantasy Relationships

Allison came to her first therapy session because a girl-friend told her she needed help. "I guess I'm depressed, but I can't tell you what's wrong," she said. She became anxious when asked if she had a boyfriend. Her eyes glazed over and welled with tears. "I haven't been lucky in love," she replied.

Graced with natural beauty, Allison dressed and bore herself in a way that didn't show off her good looks. It was surprising to discover that she had an MBA from a prestigious business school and was associated with a fine New York City firm.

She usually spoke flatly about her concerns. "I suppose my biological alarm clock is ringing. Growing up I always assumed I'd get married and have children." In the same tone, she described past relationships that amounted to a series of disappointments.

One day, however, she rushed in to describe a meeting with the head of her division. "Fred Madison is a genius! He always knows what's happening, and he can read my mind." It was startling to hear Allison speak with such intensity. "What does Fred Madison mean to you?" her therapist asked. She was stunned and pulled away. Her secret world had been penetrated. "It's something special and different. No one can ever understand how I feel about Fred Madison," she said defensively.

It was clear that Allison was deeply in love with Fred. She rarely spoke to him, but when she did, the encounter gave her a charge of emotional electricity that kept her going for days. Of course he was married, and his suburban life had a tantalizing mystique that she enjoyed in a strange way. Three years earlier, when Allison was new in the firm, Fred Madison had been her supervisor. She developed a crush on him, and at a business convention they began an intermittent affair, meeting two or three times a year.

As her trust in the therapist deepened, Allison shared more of her feelings about Fred, revealing a secret, romantic attachment that had consumed her emotions for the past three years. Allison's story may sound strange, but in fact her situation is common to many single women. She thought Fred Madison was godlike. Attractive, self-possessed, masculine, he engaged her sympathy and adoration. When he closed the door to his office, she felt protective toward him, concerned that he was overworked. When he looked in her eyes, their moments of contact "set them apart in the universe." When he advised her, a few kind words meant everything in the world. The few times they slept together were simply overwhelming to Allison, given her intense emotional connection to him. For awhile, she was glad that their trysts did not occur often, because she cherished each memory, living them over and over again in the safety and privacy of her own mind.

When Allison entered therapy, things were already changing for her. She had become depressed, for it was exhausting to subsist on crumbs, without a real relationship. Her early reluctance to discuss her attachment to Fred was a denial that protected her from looking at the relationship truthfully and seeing that it was absurd.

Afraid of real love, she was involved in a pretend relationship.

The relationship with Fred was a fantasy, devised by the part of her that longed for loving attachment. In her desire for love she latched onto a safe candidate and went through an emotional drama as if it were real. When this occurs in a woman's life, it is a manifestation of the inability to participate in a real relationship because of hidden fears.

In therapy it was necessary for Allison to face her fear of love, which was based upon her father's rejection of her. He was an intimidating, sarcastic and negative person. Allison's mother was also limited emotionally, incapable of solidness or constancy. When Allison finally stopped denying her fears and worked through the pain of her early failed attachments, she observed her new attachment to Fred Madison with perspective, appreciating her reasons for being involved in a pseudo-relationship. "I was like an orphan," she said, "and I needed a dream to keep me going. Fred was my dream, and I thought about him all of the time. By dreaming about him, I could believe that someday my dreams might come true."

Women who fear love are very susceptible to involvement in fantasy relationships. The circumstances vary, but the psychological dynamics remain the same.

Carolyn produces television commercials and travels a lot in her job. She has had many lovers, and during the first two years of therapy was involved in four very intense relationships. The difficulty with all of them was that the men lived in other cities. First there was George from Chicago. When their correspondence could no longer fan the flames of infatuation, she fell for Richard from London. Discovering six months later that he was married ruined that fantasy, so she fell for an American businessman who lived in Greece. During a year and a half they saw each other three times, but she thought of him daily and could get more emotional mileage out of one of his postcards than anyone could imagine. When he broke her heart by marrying someone else, Carolyn outdid herself in her pattern of long-distance loving: She fell for a married businessman from Australia.

Carolyn's fantasy love life illustrates a common way women create doomed relationships. They simply fall for someone who is impossible to get to know because they can never physically see one another. Often a fearful woman involves herself chronically with married men. In such cases, they may meet more frequently but there is little hope of winning them over.

Beth came to therapy following a suicide attempt. She had been the gal friday for a famous and powerful businessman in New York City. She was hypnotized by his smooth and glamorous presence. Bill, who enjoyed the ego gratification that came with getting attention from women, was a professional charmer who could turn on almost any woman. A perfect fantasy lover.

Beth worked closely with her hero, and because of the intimate nature of the work, felt she was his "wife." She made his travel arrangements, bought gifts he needed for others and handled most of his personal correspondence. In her mind the fact that he was married didn't disturb her fantasy, but it did keep him sufficiently remote for her to dream on.

Then something happened to destroy her dream and cruelly awaken her to reality. A young art director in the office began an overt flirtation with Bill, and he responded positively. After an office party they left together, and the ensuing office rumors suggested they were having an affair. Beth's depression was sudden and profound. Luckily she was rescued by a neighbor after swallowing a potential overdose of pills.

Women can stay in fantasy relationships for years. The fantasy will be destroyed only if at last they have enough courage to admit the painful reality that they are merely peripheral to the man to whom they are emotionally devoted. To keep their fantasy world intact, they must believe that he does, or will, love them— some day. These pretenses of love can center around a boss, doctor, clergyman, teacher or therapist. Surveys have indicated that more than 30% of female graduate students have affairs with their professors. And most men in the helping professions can attest to overly intense attachments on the part of their female clients. Some men derive ego gratification from this attention, and others will even take sexual advantage of the situation.

In analyzing the phenomenon of fantasy love, we could judge such attachments as a simple waste of a woman's time. But fantasy partners are signals of emotional dysfunction. Instead of considering the men in these cases as unavailable, uncommitted or otherwise blaming them for bringing heartbreak to a woman, we must see such partners as manifestations of a woman's desire for love when *she* is unavailable for love. She herself will not usually know this painful fact, for the reason she is unavailable is because of hidden, unconscious fears. Fantasy love objects are safe: They let a woman feel her loving emotions, and yet protect her from feeling her fears. No wonder they seem so wonderful!

A woman who fears love is emotionally needy. Therefore it seems like a blessing to find someone who awakens her fantasies and gives her a sense of being a desirable female. A man can seem to feed you emotionally when he charges your fantasies, and you can become addicted to the feelings he stimulates. Your constant inner refrain is: "Someday we'll be together." Actually, however, you feel safe *not* being in the mainstream of his life. Unfortunately, such attachments are not truly safe in the long run for several reasons:

- It is emotionally draining to love someone and not be loved back fully.
- It damages your self-esteem to be peripheral to someone who is central to you.
- You are stroke-starved because you exist only on emotional crumbs and your own imagination.
- You use your imagination to project good qualities on a man, many of which are your own strengths that you should own for yourself.
- Fantasy love inspires worship, which keeps you in a lowly position.
- Reality will always catch up with you, and you will feel betrayed.
- Fantasies keep you in a passive position, and you will have trouble asserting yourself in many areas of your life.

Dead-End Relationships

There is another type of relationship that protects a woman from her fear of love. This one doesn't involve a fantasy partner, but a real man with whom she is having a long-term relationship. But the relationship isn't going anywhere, and it very likely never will. You probably don't admit that it's a dead-end relationship, but act as if you are involved in something real and vital.

Rebecca had been seeing Bill for three years. They had a date every weekend and shared a beach house. Every birthday and Christmas Rebecca wondered if she might receive an engagement ring, but so far this had not happened. They never spoke of marriage, although Rebecca assumed it would come to pass someday, forever hoping for a deeper commitment. She was good to Bill, very supportive of his needs and very understanding when he couldn't reciprocate. Rebecca was always willing to swallow her pride and her desires and *wait.*

She and Bill had many friends who were married. When they went out in foursomes she behaved as if she were married to Bill. She was animated, upbeat, an excellent actress who never betrayed her disappointment. And she never confronted Bill, because she didn't want to upset him.

Single women like Rebecca get stuck in relationships that come to mean very little to either person. These relationships are way stations, filling a vacuum until you are ready for something real. It's not easy to give up a nonrelationship in favor of something scary—a real one.

When you are involved in a nonrelationship you can control it as you do a fantasy, because you invented it. You feel safe because you're one step removed from the man—you're not married. You are reluctant to give up the relationship, because so much energy has been spent on it. But it is mainly the energy of being a good actress, as well as the stamina required to keep a lid on your own wants and desires. When involved in nonrelationships, women admit to having unsatisfying sex and faking orgasms, all ways of staying invulnerable.

When you give up a safe but empty relationship you may be shocked at how little either of you is hurt by the parting. This is because there is so little to miss. You might even feel a surprising elation when you end such a depressing rut of noncontact. But only when you explore what makes you fearful of genuine loving feelings will you go on to find something real.

A woman who denies her fear of love lives in an emotional twilight zone. She tries to love another person, but she can only love her own fantasies. She may go through the motions of loving a man, but her deepest emotions do not connect to him. She is simply unable to give her love, and instead substitutes an introverted offering to some love object in her mind. Because of her hidden fears, she cannot move ahead in a relationship that increases in intimacy. Her relationships are transitional loves, like a teenager's crush on a teacher.

Unfortunately, you can waste a lot of time in transition, spending years waiting for the real thing that never comes along. If you want to get married, give up the passivity of fantasy life. Give up your naiveté about where your present relationship stands. Stop pretending! You must get out of the dependent mode in which you are expecting something magical to happen like it does in the movies. Movies are fantasies too.

Beware of the following:

- long-distance relationships
- married men
- elusive men
- Butterfly Collectors*
- men you have just met
- secret crushes
- part-, part-, part-time affairs
- sexually fantasizing about men
- maritally fantasizing about men
- passionately loving someone you barely know
- imagining the future
- dead-end relationships
- waiting, dreaming, longing

Some of the most crashing, painful lows are experienced when you discover that you have essentially invented the whole thing in your mind.

Part-Time Partners

Megan, who is thirty-four, lives with a man part-time. Jeff is divorced and has shared custody of the children of his former marriage. From Monday to Friday noon Megan works in New York City, but from Friday to

---

*Butterfly Collectors are men who prey upon women who live on crumbs and fantasy. They can have as many as a dozen women in love with them at the same time.

Monday morning she lives with Jeff in his country home. During the weekends she is, for all purposes, Jeff's wife. They entertain together, nurture the children, go out, talk, make love. The relationship is in a workable, fixed pattern, but it's static. For nearly a year it has stayed virtually the same. The problem is Megan: She's in pain because what she has with Jeff is no longer enough.

Megan and many other single women are struggling with dissatisfaction with what are essentially part-time marriages. Loving Jeff had resulted in her structuring the relationship to suit his needs. Although it seemed to work for the first few months, she soon became silently dissatisfied.

Luckily, Megan took the next step of admitting to herself where she really stood emotionally: She wanted to marry Jeff. She believed in her heart that marriage was the preferable route, and she honestly believed it was not all right not to be married to Jeff. The attachment was too important to her to be represented by a part-time affair. She stated her position clearly: "We have too much potential depth and commitment not to join our lives together. I love our time together so much that I want more. I want to take the rest of life's journey together, with you. If you won't do it, it will break my heart and yours too. But without marriage, I am leaving."

Many a woman is faced with Megan's dilemma. When she made her announcement to Jeff it was with the full knowledge that she might be ending things. When a woman says she is leaving, she must act on her threat. Whatever the outcome, she must keep asking herself, "Why should a woman like me who wants to get married stay involved with a man who doesn't?" Self-respect tells her that however deep the bond, it is time to unglue it before the pain usurps all of the pleasure. Temporary arrangements are usually unsatisfactory because long-term joy and pleasure come from depth and commitment. Not believing she deserves a deep relationship can keep a woman from going after it. Taking a stand for marriage is what many single women must do.

When you give up on dead-end relationships, you may notice there are other potential partners for you. You may also notice an upsurge of fear in yourself. Considering relationships that could actually go somewhere may feel risky. Yet if you start to feel this anxiety when you stop pretending, it's actually a good sign. Your hidden fears are no longer hidden and you can work them through by talking about them, identifying them. Expressing them will make you free of their spell. The goal is to find and overcome those unconscious blocks that stand in the way of your getting closer to a real partner.

·9·
CATCH ME IF YOU CAN

There are many ways that hidden fears of love influence women beside choosing doomed relationships. In addition to making poor choices, a woman who is afraid of her love impulses will actively avoid men who are genuine candidates for marriage. She probably isn't aware of it, but she carefully steers clear of real contacts that could lead to something meaningful.

The Elusive Woman

The woman who says that she longs for a man but cannot find him doesn't think of herself as elusive. She refuses to admit *her* unavailability. One woman said, "I check men out real quickly." What she meant was that she crossed them off her list before she had a chance to know them at all.

Women who are elusive are easily annoyed by men, using these negative emotions to create distance. Negativity offers a blanket of protection for the woman who fears love. She quickly gets upset about things that displease her, and is afraid to focus on qualities that are likable in a man. Many psychologists are convinced that when a woman is irritated with a man, it's a sign that the two are getting close. A fearful woman refuses to work through differences, denying she cares for the man. She ends things instead of fighting normal lovers' quarrels, because those skirmishes more often than not will lead to heightened intimacy and new levels of mutual understanding. The fearful woman breaks contact just when there are opportunities for getting closer, just when things are getting good.

One manifestation of a woman's fear of love is a kind of vagueness in her personality. She is afraid to declare herself, to be who she really is. Because she is not sharply defined, it's hard for a man—or anyone else—to make contact with her. She remains elusive.

By contrast, a woman who is ready for mating is a differentiated woman: unique, different from her family and everyone else as well. Such a woman is sure of herself. She presents herself to a man not as an elusive being, but as a solid person he can deal with. A confident woman is not afraid to be clear about what she expects to get in a relationship: appreciation, trust, love and comfort.

A woman develops maturity as her positive self-image gets stronger, as she really comes to like her own unique characteristics. Such positive confidence and self-awareness develop through interactive relationships: We discover ourselves through the reflected appraisal of others. We can mature in our identity through friendships and work relationships that give us a real sense of who we are.

You should begin right away to be more outspoken, expressing your likes and dislikes clearly. If you aren't used to doing this, begin to make yourself known in small ways. It will become much easier as you go along. The more you let people see how unique you are, the more risks you'll be able to take. When you are clearly defined and not elusive, the easier you'll be to catch! You'll also be able to attract someone on the same wavelength; men won't need to keep guessing—perhaps wrongly—about what you're really like.

FINDING REAL PROSPECTS

When a woman is elusive but doesn't know it, she thinks it's the men who are always trying to get away. She conveys a special kind of reserve, and it's not the same as playing the clever game of hard-to-get. Though she might be the first to deny it, she gives the message loud and clear that she isn't available for anything serious. Men who are afraid of closeness themselves will know they are safe with her, that the relationship won't go anywhere. An elusive woman doesn't see that real prospects are there all the time, and instead might focus on a man who is a confirmed bachelor. He may be attractive and successful, but he is narcissistically wrapped up in himself and is dating her precisely *because* she will not press for marriage.

The real marriage prospect is different. He's a regular

guy. What distinguishes him as a potential partner are not his accomplishments, his looks or his savvy (although he could have all that and more), but his capacity to bond with you as a mate. An elusive woman is naive about what qualities make a good partner, discounting any real prospects because of her "high standards." If you are harboring a secret fear of love, whatever a man is *not* is what you will prefer. We've heard all the excuses, from "I only like very successful men" to "I'm only attracted to men with dark hair."

A Loveless Script

Early in childhood we reached conclusions about ourselves, about others and about the quality of life. Your conclusions may be realistic or illusory, but you arrived at them through the experiences of your childhood, and they help form the script that identifies your role in life.

Put simply, if you were adored and catered to, you might have come to the conclusion that you are a queen and the world is your oyster. On the other hand, if you were mistreated or ignored, you might have concluded that you are inadequate and life is a drag. These conclusions are the foundation of your script, and you live life accordingly. Once started, a script builds on itself and becomes firmly set. We look for evidence to prove our early conclusions and we discard any evidence to the contrary. The system reinforces itself: New experiences are translated in ways that make them feel like repetitions of our early experiences.

Are you living a spontaneous life or following an old

script? If you are living out a script, the same miserable things seem to happen over and over again. You are tied to painful emotions and can't release yourself from them. If you are living a real life, there are surprises and new adventures along the way, all kinds of emotions that ebb and flow, and you don't get stuck on an old familiar path of emotional pain.

A script gives you a rigid sense of how things *should* be, even if circumstances don't conform to your expectations. In real life there's room for the unexpected, and you are surprised by some of the twists and turns your life takes. If you're living a script, you stubbornly refuse to admit spontaneity and newness in order to minimize emotional risks.

Perhaps your loveless script was written when you heard your mother saying how unhappy she was in her marriage. You looked around and saw that her sisters felt the same way. If, in addition, your father was remote and your own boyfriend was hopelessly immature, you were well on your way to developing a loveless life script.

You absorbed these experiences and arrived at an unexpressed—and unchallenged—conclusion: "Marriage is the pits. Men are impossible. I can't be happy with a man." This became your script on men. Of course, it then becomes self-fulfilling.

You stay wedded to a bad script because the painful emotional burdens of the past were so powerful that you simply can't believe in any other reality. If your mother was desperately unhappy in her marriage, you were brainwashed by someone whose feelings were more important to you than anyone in the world. As an adult you've left the actual situation behind, but you haven't outgrown the conditioning to follow it.

A loveless script is like a prison sentence in which you aren't allowed to have love in your life. It works out that way too because you look at everything in life from the script's frame of reference. You look for people and experiences to confirm your belief in the loveless quality of life, creating your own reality through selective perception, only allowing yourself to see things that support your preconceived view.

What are your basic beliefs about yourself, about other people and about the quality of life? The key to understanding your own script is to discover whether there is a repetitive, loveless pattern in your life that involves not only events but a recurring, painful emotion. The initial "scripting" experience usually occurred in your childhood, and similar problems in relationships mysteriously seem to repeat themselves later on. This is because you bring to all your relationships an emotional readiness to feel that old, familiar pain. Is one of these loveless scripts yours?

All Men Will Abandon Me

If your parents were divorced you may be so ready for abandonment that you have anxiety when your boyfriend is on a business trip. You can feel threatened by abandonment even if you have a loyal partner. Be careful of your tendency to look for unreliable men.

All Men Are Disappointing

With this script you either pick men who are losers or are highly critical of any man when you spot a weakness in him. This script makes it difficult to know who would be a good partner because you can always spot some "fatal" flaw. You must learn to leave your past disappointments behind you. This woman may have had a disappointing father or one who was so wonderful no other man could ever hope to match him.

All Men Are Insensitive

This belief is common in women whose mothers were unable to form a sensitive give-and-take relationship in their own marriages. You must learn to be a good communicator, and discover the sensitivity that a man can possess when you reach out for it. It is crucial that you connect with well-meaning men.

All Men Are Womanizers

If your father left your mother, or someone left you for another woman, you will fear this happening again. Ironically, women who have dated a married man and later married him are especially plagued with this fear. Any unfounded jealousy and paranoia can be destructive to a relationship, and often professional help is necessary to resolve these emotions. You must stay clear of men with reputations as womanizers.

No Man Will Ever Love Me

Lacking enough loving attention in childhood can lead you to negativity and hopelessness—neither of which will attract love in the present. If someone has let you down in the past, you will be tempted to protect yourself by retreating from intimacy.

The elusive female plays a game of catch-me-if-you-can, in support of her script. By not seeing a man's good qualities and focusing on his weaknesses, she continuously reinforces her beliefs. If she quickly finds fault with men, she's just confirming the inner voice that tells her all men are disappointing. If she is easily annoyed, that proves no man can ever make her happy.

Scripts are tragic because they keep you so narrow that you have no concept of what is possible between men and women who pledge to love each other and grow together. But there is an option to a loveless life: Consider the possibility of living in a way that is less self-protected. Being negative and hopeless about love creates a safe little cave, but you really aren't safe in it. Your growth is limited. You are lonely and not having much fun. A negative script was forced on you by circumstances, but pessimism is not a natural way to think or to live. It's possible to change your loveless script, and the place to start is in your attitudes toward men. You probably deny the part of yourself that likes men; women in loveless scripts always have many negative things to say about them.

Take inventory of what you think about men in your own mind and what you say about them when you talk to other people. Practice tuning into positive feelings toward men, thinking about what it is you like about each man you know. This is a first step in challenging a loveless script, which is primarily reinforced by finding fault with men.

Too Good to Be True: The Magic Gesture

Everyone has an endearing part of the personality that is like a child, expressive of humor, warmth and creativity. Yet the child in us also can be timid, fearful and vulnerable. If you have been mistreated or neglected emotionally, your inner child will lack self-confidence. Mistreatment and neglect are profoundly damaging to self-esteem, and a little girl who is not sufficiently loved will wonder if this means that there's something wrong with her to cause her parents to feel unloving toward her. Even asking herself this question can be devastating to her ego, so she formulates a plan to reverse her fate. She resolves to be a good girl, and prove that she is worthy of being loved.

Like Cinderella, another good but neglected girl, she sings "When You Wish Upon a Star," believing in the magical wish that if only she is good enough, someday her prince will come. That's the real motivation behind so many single women's incredible "goodness." Experts in the art of people-pleasing, they remember to send birthday cards to everyone and in general can be the most thoughtful people in the world. Friends wonder why they are single, because they have so much to offer and give so much!

Freud spoke of this phenomenon in describing the daughter of one of his friends. The little girl was being especially affectionate toward her father, and someone remarked what a loving child she was. Freud's further interpretation was that she was enacting the way she wanted to be loved herself. He called it "the magic gesture"—the belief that your own loving acts will magically come your way.

Of course, the spiritual principle of being good as a way to bring goodness to oneself doesn't always work, when there are other realities at play beneath the surface of this dynamic. Often the good person simply gets stuck in proving her worthiness of love over and over. She gets involved in relationships that require the patience of a saint because they don't go anywhere. She also has the hidden fear of receiving love from someone else and thus establishes one-way relationships. She has found a way never to be vulnerable to another person's rejection by taking charge completely of her own self-esteem. She has gone to such an extreme of proving her own goodness that she doesn't make herself vulnerable to love. She is deeply afraid of falling in love and losing these defenses.

Maryanne was working on giving up her rigidity in therapy. She wanted to let herself be more yielding emotionally, to really love a man. She came for treatment precisely at the point in a relationship when her long-term boyfriend began to get very serious. She'd complained for years that he wouldn't marry her, but when he went through some personal growth and found that he wanted a real commitment, Maryanne panicked and began having fantasies of breaking up with him. She was comfortable as a devoted, long-suffering part-time lover, but now John wanted more from her and she realized she needed to learn true responsiveness. With her therapist's support, Maryanne finally allowed herself to be loved by John.

The theme of goodness is an important one to understand in yourself. Clarissa fell in love with Andy three years ago. She was the youngest in a large family with too few emotional resources. When Andy came into her life, he awakened many of her unmet needs and she began to feel like a child at times. He loved her, and was committed to marrying her when they both got out of graduate school, but she panicked and became obsessed with the fear that it wouldn't work out.

At one point in treatment Clarissa had a telling fantasy. "What if he leaves me?" she asked. She imagined a whole scenario, picturing Andy getting tired of her and finally rejecting her. As she imagined him mysteriously drifting away, she felt a terrible pain—followed by a strange detachment. She then fantasized becoming a nun, zealously devoted to helping sick people in a hospital. "That's it!" she exclaimed. "If he leaves me I'll drop out of school and become a nurse-nun." She imagined herself being so good that she couldn't possibly have deserved being left. In reality, Andy didn't leave her. They are married now, with their first child.

Clarissa's fantasy holds an important clue about lovelessness and how people seek self-reassurance when they've been emotionally neglected. The fear that something is wrong with you is so terribly threatening that you make an emotional decision to give up on fulfilling your own needs, and instead be a servant of others in need. Of course such giving is worthy and admirable, but it would be much better to give from a full cup instead of an empty one.

Rigidly "good" people are often too out of touch with their own needs to go after what they really want. The neediness they conceal with their seeming generosity creates a one-dimensional aspect to their personalities that keeps their relationships from ever becoming real and fulfilling. Such people can be *too* good, and will be taken advantage of.

Elizabeth bestowed her goodness on Richard and he

loved it. She clipped timely articles on his business and sent them to him, charmed him with special little treats like Belgian chocolates for his sweet tooth and a rare album of his favorite jazz group. The trouble was, she contacted him with only one side of herself: the unselfish, giving side. When she decided to express some of her own needs, he didn't like the change in her. He complained she was putting too much pressure on him. Their initial contact had been based on her being generous and good. Elizabeth was a true Cinderella, promising never to show him her "down" side—or her needs—after midnight.

The problem with being so good is that you never learn how to be real in a relationship. This keeps you from being loved as you really are. Unfortunately, your good behavior will be rewarded in your friendships, with your devotion to being good reinforcing a negative cycle. Married couples often play fairy godmother to wonderful single women. They are so touched by her goodness, they want to move in and play matchmaker. They include her in their lives, rely on her companionship, her help with parties, babysitting, etc.

Gail was "adopted" by several couples during the time we knew her in therapy. The last couple she spent considerable time with didn't like it when she became more self-assertive and less adaptable to whatever they wanted from her. They had loved her "goodness" but now criticized her "selfishness." After their falling out, Gail met Ron. From the beginning she was less giving and more self-respecting than had been her pattern with relationships in the past. Ron adjusted himself to her. "I'm not as nice anymore, yet people are nicer to me,"

Gail observed. "Except for those who still expect me to be a little Goody Two-shoes."

NOBODY IS A SAINT

If we take a serious look at this caricature of goodness, we must realize that there is a flip side to the coin. What is the other side of goodness? Nobody is a saint, and if you try desperately to be good to a fault, you will inevitably experience anger and resentment toward those who don't match your selflessness. The intolerance that goodness produces can go a long way in keeping you and other good women from getting married.

When you try so hard, you end up feeling cheated, and so become stingy in your approval of others. Such giving is not generosity so much as the self-serving desire to magically induce others to treat you in the same way. If you're so good, how could anyone not love you? If you must manipulate and control your image in the world in this way, you'll never allow others to confront you with your less desirable traits or grow as a person. This is the theme of so many of Barbara Pym's novels about "excellent women" (one of her titles) who remain spinsters.

Almost everyone struggles with the fear of being unlovable at some point in their lives. Rather than mask this fear with compulsive goodness, it's better to face it. There *is* such a thing as unconditional love—you *can* be loved as a whole person, but it must include your weaknesses as well as your strengths. In fact, real people with some weaknesses are much easier to take than paragons of perfection. They're lovable.

Psychological or spiritual counseling can be very helpful in learning to love and accept yourself without perfectionistic standards. This is the groundwork for establishing a loving and intimate relationship with a partner from whom there is no hidden or unexpressed side of yourself. In order to get married, you must learn to accept your man with both his weaknesses and strengths, and the first step in this process is accepting your own full range of emotions and characteristics.

·10·
OVERCOMING THE
FEAR OF MEN

At one point in our research on why so many single women are having trouble getting married, we asked ourselves whether on some level they just don't like men. We reasoned that millions of women *are* able to get married. Even women with lots of shortcomings somehow manage to find committed partners.

We discovered that the majority of our single women patients looking for partners tend to love men very much. They describe intensely romantic attachments, past and present. They speak of men they care for with appreciation of their best qualities. They are capable of generosity, and have the capacity for joyful intimacy. They are often quite free and expressive sexually. That's why at first we were so baffled by their dilemma. Their friends and family reinforce this view, and also wonder why such lovely, loving women don't have the husbands they say they want. Slowly we recognized that such women resist mating.

In therapy this type of woman is often confused. She feels like a victim of something she doesn't understand. If she isn't too demoralized, she'll say that she's a good, loving person, that she'd love to have a supportive husband, but that some kind of irrational fate directs her love life. She feels condemned, prohibited from having something she wants to have more than anything. Simplistic self-help strategies are absurd and insulting to her, because she's attractive, charming, kind to men. Yes, she loves men every bit as much as women who have husbands—but her inner, hidden enemy is fear of men. It's particularly hard for such a woman to consider that the "man-shortage" theory is a coverup for her fear.

This chapter is about how you can understand and overcome your unconscious resistance, which is based on fear. Resistance is a natural, primitive force that kicks into action whenever your psyche concludes that your emotional safety or well-being is at stake. It is irrational and very powerful. Resistance shows itself in such observable behavior as avoidance, testiness, withdrawal or confusion. Women who have hidden fears based on painful love experiences in the past become resistant whenever a man threatens to get too close emotionally. Resistance emerges even when the man is wonderful and would be just right for her, posing no seeming threat. Why? In getting closer to him, she lets down her defenses and thus stirs up her painful past experiences and the fears she has tried to hide from herself by years of denial.

Actually, you have good reasons for your resistance. Most single women have developed independent lifestyles to protect them from hurt, even though they don't

protect them from loneliness. You guard your independence as a safe haven against being overwhelmed
or demoralized in a relationship.

You can be quite terrified by the passionate neediness
that surfaces when you let a man get really close to you.
And you are vulnerable to the bursting of those flood-
gates when you've been needy for a long time—perhaps
a lifetime. Because your loving experiences haven't
lasted, you build a strong wall around yourself to keep
out the possibility of more pain. In spite of your loving
nature, you hold tight to the grim belief that you shouldn't
count on anyone but yourself.

Androphobia: The Problem without a Name

The emotional problem that keeps single women from
getting married is fear. Your very tendency to love a
man deeply makes you vulnerable to being hurt. Love
and pain have become so closely connected in your
psyche that avoidance of men is the only way you know
how to protect yourself.

At times, your intense desire for love can't be fully
suppressed, so you indulge in safe love, unconsciously
choosing relationships that have built-in endings. A
woman who loves men must indulge her loving feelings
occasionally. But if your safe lover actually becomes
available for a commitment, an enormous terror or even
despair surfaces.

Seeing this happen again and again in the lives of our
single women patients has made us certain that such a
pattern governs their lives to a paralyzing degree. We

have named the problem androphobia, from the Greek *andros* (man) and *phobia* (fear). Androphobia is the fear a woman has of commitment because she is terrified of getting hurt. She is in touch with her feelings of love, and sometimes with her pain. But she is *unaware* that she avoids commitment, considering it a trapdoor leading to emotional devastation. She is unaware that her own behavior keeps relationships at a distance. The androphobic woman's psyche is unconsciously working to keep her safe from love's harm.

Androphobia consists of both the belief that love will inevitably lead to pain, and a set of phobic behaviors in which a woman avoids love leading to marriage through her "safe" choices. Because of anxiety and fear, androphobic women avoid intimacy. That's why they're never attracted to men who are available for committed love and marriage. They may say that the men they know are all unattractive or otherwise unsuitable, but unconsciously they are behaving like the agoraphobic woman who avoids shopping malls by rationalizing that shopping malls are not as attractive as boutiques and that they offer only inferior goods. Secretly, however, it's containment of fear and anxiety that really motivates her to favor a small shop and to avoid the mall (or the airport or the supermarket).

Avoiding anxiety, making the "safe" choice, sensing relief. That's the phobic pattern, and it explains why women who otherwise love and desire men very much stay single. In order to be relieved from her anxiety about the hurt that can result from intimacy, the androphobic woman curbs her deep instinct to love and bond with a partner. She may indeed love the idea of loving another, but her fear, operating unconsciously, is greater. Actually, she has a many-layered neurosis. Pretending to be without fear is part of the protective shell of any phobic person: In addition to a specific fear (of heights, of men), the phobic person also fears their fear.

For this reason, it's vital for the androphobic woman to honestly recognize her fear of loving a man. Instead of blaming the singles culture, or complaining of the seeming lack of appropriate men, *admit to yourself that you are afraid of getting really close to a man.* This admission has been the turning point for many single women in our practices. Abandoning your denial, owning up to your fear puts you in charge, because you can't do much to change men or the culture, but you *can* work on yourself.

Begin by carefully examining your history in love. You will probably find ample support for your fears. *Stop pretending you aren't fearful of men.* It's time to stop being fooled by your own bravado. The fact is that deep intimacy is terrifying to you, and it threatens to deluge you with pain and sadness that has been neatly repressed in your unconscious for a long time.

In therapy sessions with our women patients, we found issues that came up again and again, and we developed a profile of the androphobic woman.

An androphobic woman:

- fears repeating her mother's marriage
- experienced a distant or angry father
- is emotionally detached, with a low-grade depression

- had one or more bad relationships with men, including losses through death or divorce
- spends more time with women than with men
- has a tendency to be involved with unavailable men
- compartmentalizes any relationship with a man, fiercely defending her independence.

Some of these characteristics may hit home for you. Understanding the specific dynamics of your fear will help you to release the power they have over you. Released from unconscious fear, you can find freedom to love and to commit yourself to something permanent.

Breaking the Cycle of Fear

In this section we will discuss each aspect of our profile of the androphobic woman. Some of these issues have been discussed earlier, such as the effect of negative parental relationships on the ability to love fully. We will focus here on understanding both how you learned fear and how you maintain it. This understanding can help you let go of your phobic beliefs and your phobic avoidance of commitment. You must work to consciously recognize your unconscious beliefs. You must accept the fact that your androphobia is a protective mechanism. You must relinquish the power past experiences still have over you. You must reconsider your conclusions—All men are like Dad, or George, or Sam. Marriage means being like my mother. Love always hurts, etc. Finally, you must stop making the destructive choices you always make and let go of the confirmed loneliness that results from your beliefs about love inevitably leading to pain.

THE FEAR OF REPEATING MOTHER'S MARRIAGE

How does a little girl envision her future? Mostly within the framework of her mother's life. The mother-daughter relationship is more than an attachment to someone who takes care of you; it involves your very identity. You once believed that you would grow up to be just like Mother, as if no other choices were conceivable. Your mother was your future self.

Many androphobic women have androphobic mothers who married but lived in fear of their husbands, structuring a whole lifestyle based on their fears.

Your mother's fear of your father was basic to your family system. Yet your father may not have been the monster your mother made him out to be, because the original agent of *her* conditioning could have been her own father or grandfather. One severely fear-provoking ancestor can spawn generations of fearful women. Whatever the original cause, you watched your mother walk on eggshells, obsessed with avoiding your father's disapproval, fearful of provoking him in any way. This helped create, or at least maintain, the husband behaving like a male monster.

Your mother instructed you in the classic principles of androphobia: Don't ask your father's permission for anything before he has eaten his dinner; don't tell him I spent this much money on the dress; let's not show him your report card. There was also avoidance of his presence, conversations that stopped dead when he appeared, hours of mute tiptoeing around the house while he read or rested—a family life that went on not with him, but in spite of him or around him. Compulsively serving your father as if he were a baby, your mother was afraid to stop this behavior.

Beth told how her mother stayed up all night cooking a week's worth of meals and freezing them so she could go to her sister's deathbed and not be chided for neglecting her wifely duties. Claudia told of her father complaining when he opened an untidy closet; in fearful obedience her mother became a compulsive housekeeper. Afraid that someone would "upset" her husband, your mother became anxious if the baby cried, a two-year-old felt cranky or a teenager got hysterical over a failed hairdo. It's easy to see how a little girl growing up in this situation would learn to fearfully avoid men.

Growing up with an androphobic mother, you also saw her anger, but it was only expressed covertly—by irritating her husband, henpecking him, sabotaging his morale. You watched her tempt fate by deliberately overspending his hard-earned money, being wildly disorganized or daring to overwhelm him with emotional problems at the very moment he would be most frustrated.

This was how the fearful woman rebelled. She wanted to see her husband lose his cool from time to time, in revenge for the tyranny of fear that controlled her life and, more importantly, as a reminder of horrible "male" explosions. By provoking him, she "proved" that her life of fearing her husband was justified, that her fear was her husband's fault. She didn't take responsibility for her own beliefs, attitudes or behaviors that encouraged and supported this dynamic. Androphobic mothers, whether in their servile or irritating modes, dehumanize their husbands into fear objects.

When you grow up with an androphobic mother, you empathize with her feelings of victimization. You wish she was free of her diminished way of living. With the coming of feminism, you finally had support in rejecting female servility. At the age of independence, you not only separated from home, but you also probably rejected your mother's whole lifestyle.

But the androphobic script remained. An ironic *unconscious to conscious* exchange occurred. The mother who was consciously fearful of her husband was unconsciously desirous of self-development. Today, her daughter is consciously self developed but unconsciously harbors deep fears of men. She may not know that there is a way to be intimate with a man without resorting to the servile behaviors of her fearful mother. Remaining single, the daughter of an androphobic mother hasn't addressed the problem of relating to a man without fear. She has simply avoided it.

In working on your resistance to intimacy, be aware of the dynamics of fear between your mother and father, and be completely honest as to how bad it was. As a child, did you see the situation at home in terms of a big, bad father and a sweet, accommodating mother? Did you learn an androphobic response by identifying with your mother, feeling protective toward her? Did you have conversations in which she unburdened herself concerning her unhappiness over her relationship with your father? Once conditioned to fear men, you will let fear operate like an automatic reflex in your psyche. If your mother lived by fear, you probably do too.

After making these connections to your own history, one of the most useful things you can do is become aware of a different way of operating with a man. Your mother could have been less of a victim if she had known how to be more assertive. You can loosen the fear response connected to this fixed image of your servile mother by realizing that, like most obsequious behaviors, hers was not forced upon her but was one of her own emotional interactional habits learned in childhood.

Next, begin to observe the way self-respecting women relate to their husbands. They don't baby them, rescue them or compulsively cater to them. They candidly share their feelings and perceptions about things, and openly communicate about what is important to them. These unfearful women don't have to prove anything through trying a man's patience either. Not being an object of fear, he is seen by them as a real person to be loved and cared for.

A self-respecting woman might make some of the same caring gestures that your mother did, but she gives to her partner from the fullness of her love, not from fear. What will probably be most striking to you in your observations about such a woman is the extent to which she includes her partner in her life. He is not someone to be avoided, but is invited to share her concerns and to participate in her activities.

THE FEAR OF A DISTANT OR ANGRY FATHER

We cannot overemphasize the significance of your early relationship to your father in determining your future success in marriage. It is especially hard to be honest about how he negatively affected you if you loved him a lot. Even if he gave everyone the silent treatment, or had outbursts of temper that upset everyone, you might tell yourself that nothing he did was all that bad. It hurts too much to remember your true feelings.

Noble, loving sentiments can fool you about the hidden psychic link you make between love and pain. This association is difficult to unravel later on. You may be forced to avoid love altogether if love and pain are inextricably associated in your mind. Given this psychological linkage, letting yourself love is pure masochism.

Be honest about your father's behavior. Outbursts of temper and acts of violence strike at deep fears in anyone, short-circuiting the human psyche. A little girl needs love and closeness with her father to optimize her development as a growing person. It's terribly upsetting if your father is distant, hostile or downright cruel or unloving on an on-going basis. It's very likely that later you will generalize experiences with your father to include all other men. Fear of repeating those painful experiences leads you to a systematic, albeit unconscious, avoidance of intimacy.

In coming to terms with your androphobia, it's important that you know what particular sensitivity or trauma your avoidance is about. Because you needed a close and loving relationship with your father when you were growing up, neglect is just as traumatic as abuse. Sophie described how her father planned for her brother to go to law school but didn't care if she, his talented daughter, went to college. Diana wept remembering a scarf her father once gave her. For so many years she had longed for his attention that when she got this token present from him she felt a very intense emotion. Amelia remembered feeling sad yet angry at her obese, depressed father who characteristically slumped in his chair and rarely spoke. These women are victims of neglectful fathers.

Abuse is equally destructive to the father-daughter bond. Lynn remembered proudly wearing a tight red sweater over her first bra and having her irate father slap her in the face and call her a slut. Tara recalled her father blowing up at her when the house was messy—because her mother was too sick to keep things clean. Francine's father would grill her about current events, telling her she was stupid when correct answers were not forthcoming.

Fragments of painful memories must be unearthed, their psychic toxins released and their meaning reassessed in the light of adulthood. In therapy with an androphobic woman there are special moments of truth in which a painful memory of Dad is experienced, then released from the unconscious. Because traumas make you shut down, you must open the doors that have been closed, thawing those frozen memories, feeling those emotions that got scared right out of you. Tears often accompany this opening-up process. They are tools for healing because ultimately they express not sadness, but acceptance. Feeling and then accepting the past is the first step in allowing yourself to move on.

REPEATING THE PAST

Some androphobic women who suffered abuse or neglect from their fathers avoid intimacy altogether. Others develop a compulsion to repeat the trauma by entering into relationships that mirror the past. A common result of trauma is that it fixes you psychologically in the traumatic relationship. What therapists call the repetition compulsion is your unconscious need to repeat the situation like a broken record with the irrational hope of finally getting it right—getting the happy ending you deserved in order to be able to move on from your father's love to another man's affection. Often what is labeled as masochism in a woman is her attempt to make it right with Dad through someone like him.

We are concerned with the cycle of being unloved that is established in these cases. You *can* avoid love to avoid pain, but you end up with pain anyway, because you feel so lonely. And if you unconsciously try to work things out with a man like Dad, you risk re-creating the original pain.

When you have recognized and felt the pain of your unrewarding relationship with Dad, it's time to try some new experiences. One of the best corrective experiences for androphobia is a good friendship with a man. This may be new territory for you, so a word of caution is in order: Reject the temptation to become romantically involved with a man who seems older, wiser and stronger. When you look for a peer, an equal, you resist repeating the past. Our women patients who got married in spite of big problems with their fathers found someone who was a true friend, who didn't play power games with them, who didn't neglect or bully them. Such a man will inspire your trust, allowing you to grow beyond the painful conditioning of your childhood.

EMOTIONAL DETACHMENT AND LOW-GRADE DEPRESSION

In working with women who love yet fear men, we are often struck by the sadness in their eyes, reflecting their mourning. It's as if they've been forced to detach themselves from something they want very much. It was snatched from them, like a beloved person who died.

Vivian felt depressed whenever she saw a couple embracing in the park where she jogged. Once she reported being deeply upset after seeing a couple kissing on a subway platform. But most of the time her mood was dull. She was blanketed in a low-grade depression, emotionally detached from her unhappiness at not having the husband she wanted.

Depression results from putting a lid on vital emotions. It can be psychologically useful at times, blunting the sharp pain of grief—after the death of a loved one, for instance. It's also a way to give your psyche a rest in difficult moments, but as an ongoing emotional habit, depression will keep you feeling half alive.

Androphobic depression can take a manic form. Some women throw themselves into flurries of activity as a diversion from their depression. The degree of hyperactivity is a clue to the extent of a depression. Are you overscheduled with exercise classes, a demanding job, socializing and travel? These are healthy alternatives to a depressed funk at times, but problems will occur when your activities don't reflect what you really want to be doing and are instead ways to avoid what you are really feeling.

Sad eyes are an important clue. Framed in an otherwise animated face and body, the contrasting depression in a woman's eyes is striking. Bernadette, an otherwise lively looking interior decorator, recognized this within herself: "Ever since my divorce three years ago, I've had dreary eyes."

It might sound strange, but the women whose pain we are describing aren't very emotional. They avoid their feelings, and their early therapy sessions revolve around issues at work. When they tentatively begin to discuss their feelings, a certain grimness surfaces as they struggle with whether or not they want to be in touch with the pain they are covering up.

You may be hiding under a protective cloud of depression, or avoiding unhappiness with overactivity. But don't be afraid to touch base with the sadness inside. Let the pain of unmet desires surface, and let yourself feel the jealousy you harbor for others who have what you want. Remember the passionate attachments you had that didn't work out. You may feel that you're being immature when you give in to sadness, anger and other memories of the men you've loved. But releasing these feelings into consciousness allows you to move forward emotionally. Your struggle to be "nice" and "perfect" and "good" will make it tough to own up to the darker feelings humans have always felt, but admitting them finally will make you softer, more real—and therefore attractive.

ONE OR MORE BAD RELATIONSHIPS WITH MEN

Fear is learned when you experience pain. The most important thing you can do is to take inventory of your past relationships with men, not in the interest of building a case for how impossible relationships are, but in order to let them go. You are better off mourning your losses and feeling your pain than in suppressing those feelings, because it is your unexpressed feelings that run your life. That's why psychotherapy, with its encouragement of truthful expression, allows people to let go of the past and move on to new experiences. People who smugly feel they can handle heavy emotions by ignoring them are misguided, naive and tellingly self-protective. Ignoring the past puts you in its grip. Denial and avoidance where love is concerned will screen out present and future possibilities for love.

You can do what many of our patients have done—review emotional memories and release them. Anita remembered her former husband of six years, whose affair with a mutual friend had broken her trust. Ellen remembered her college boyfriend, whose child she had and then gave up for adoption. Beverly remembered her husband, who was killed in Vietnam. Judith remembered the pain of separating from her beloved father because of her parents' divorce when she was seven.

Opening up memories means mourning your losses. You must cry out all the tears. There *is* a finite quantity of them, even though it might not seem so. The grief of separation, of dreams gone sour, of the death of a relationship shouldn't be repressed. Focusing on the negative ("I'm glad he's gone"), burying the pain or carrying on while denying it—these all leave the past hurt unresolved. Release your sadness, if you want to be ready to make a place in your heart for the love you need.

It's difficult to love after you've been hurt. Heartbreak is an inoculation against love. When you fully appreciate this, you will begin to take the pressure off yourself. Staying super-strong, you hold back from intimacy. Understand your history, feel your disappointments, shed some tears. This is the only way to let the past go.

If a person who was close to you has died—mother, father, brother, sister, spouse or child—you are particularly susceptible to androphobia. After suffering a loved one's death, you risk generalizing the pain of loss, making you unable to love again with commitment. Spontaneous and complete loving will feel distinctly unsafe.

Almost as difficult is overcoming an abusive experience with a man. The deepest fears you can feel are related to either abandonment or violence. The woman abandoned through the death of a loved one must mourn, but the woman who has suffered violence must understand that there are other men in the world who do not hate women, who can be loving and supportive. The temptation is to scapegoat all other men for what has happened to you in the past. Abuse of women by men is a traumatic experience that evokes the use of primitive defenses such as withdrawal, detachment and repression. These are ways to cope with something that's nearly impossible to handle. Being emotionally or physically abused by a man commonly results in androphobia. But a victim of violence must work it through: remember it, talk about it, express deep feelings that are pent up inside. With help, an abused woman can overcome the trauma and be free. Feeling healed from the past, you are more capable of responding without fear when a good man comes along.

SPENDING MORE TIME WITH WOMEN THAN WITH MEN

It isn't only androphobic women who find special pleasure in the company of other women. The experience
of empathy and understanding as well as the spirit
of fun is a fulfilling part of friendships between females. Life without women friends would be bleak
indeed.

The androphobic woman takes her relationships with
women a step farther, however. She trusts them, but
doesn't trust men at all. She allows women friends to
be an ongoing part of her life, but men are kept safely
on the periphery. If she dates a man occasionally, she
spends more time talking about him to her female friends
than she does talking to him. Emotional sharing takes
place exclusively with other women, and is her prime
way of communicating. Intimate connections are in-
creasingly polarized in this woman's mind. She doesn't
know that a similar level of friendship is possible with
a man, that he is human too. Her sense of what's possible with a man is unrealistically limited.

Amanda enjoys being with her girlfriends. They go
out together almost every weekend, celebrating birth-
days and promotions at work and banding together in
times of crisis. They have been a wonderful source of
support for Amanda, and she is the first to admit that
the best place to get strokes is with the girls. She has
two sisters and knows that she developed some of her
present emotional habits in childhood. While her father
and brother Sam were involved in sports, Amanda, her
mother and sisters were running their social lives and
planning the future. They still have regular conversa-

tions, and they need to filter all of life's events through this female network.

Women like Amanda have wonderful female support in their lives, but if they want to find husbands, they must break with the very women they are intimate with and enter a different—and difficult—territory. Not only will they begin to experience the other women's envy, jealousy and anger, but also their own wish to break away from "the girls," their resentment of their friends' hostility to their wish for a greater independence from them, their guilt—and, finally, their fear of men.

Developing a deep friendship with a man may not be as easy as it is with a woman, but the differences between the sexes can reward you with satisfaction. Love or friendship between a man and woman means appreciating your differences and contacting unexpressed parts of yourself that you see in him. Ironically, exploring differences rather than empathic sameness is an adventure that can lead to profound closeness. If you keep the world of men and the world of women polarized, you won't begin the journey toward intimacy with a man.

INVOLVEMENT WITH UNAVAILABLE MEN

The androphobic woman's tendency to be involved with unavailable men complicates things terribly, because it effectively reinforces her androphobic beliefs. This behavior is extremely common among single women who fear men, and we have many among our patients. They fall in love with men who live in other cities, married men, foreign citizens, compulsive playboys, confirmed bachelors, men who are too old or too young, the gay kind, mama's boys, and all other varieties of problem men—passive, ambivalent, asexual, sociopathic or misogynist. The protective, defensive part of their psyches makes these men brilliant choices, since they'll never commit themselves to women. Their "dangerous" mating instincts are skillfully diverted by a diligent unconscious mechanism that is determined to keep them safe from love's harm.

We've also seen what happens when a formerly unavailable man changes his ways and begins to look like a good prospect for a husband. In spite of her chronic complaints about being single, the androphobic woman panics when someone she cares about becomes available. This happened to Rosemary when her married boyfriend decided to divorce his wife. She had suffered deeply as the other woman, but visions of being his wife suddenly terrified her. Such a woman characteristically has a hard time with any available man who is really interested in her, compulsively looking at his faults and mentally devaluing him. The androphobic woman's fault-finding routines sabotage her desire to move closer to anyone she really loves, who starts to show real commitment to her.

Most unavailable men do not change, and it's tragic that a woman is tricked by her unconscious mind into loving someone who will eventually hurt her. Not aware of her androphobia, she lets herself get involved. A deep attachment grows because she feels the unconscious margin of safety. She lets herself love more passionately than she ever would if he were available and therefore unsafe. At some point the relationship can go no farther because of his impairment, whether it be situational or psychological. The androphobic woman then experiences abandonment and rejection. She is crushed, devastated, depressed.

Androphobia is a vicious cycle. An androphobic woman's relationships are destined to go nowhere. Instead, the original psychic pain of abandonment or rejection is repeated, and the androphobia is reinforced. It's a habit-building system that reconfirms the belief that men are not to be trusted in the first place. Understanding the dynamics of androphobia explains why an otherwise intelligent woman makes the wrong choices. How could I have been so naive about his marriage (his homosexuality, his neurosis, his narcissism, his immaturity)? You weren't naive at all—but you did skillfully pick a guy you could love *because* he was unavailable.

There is hope in the power of analysis and insight. Once you understand unconscious mechanisms, they lose some of their power to trick you. When you find yourself painfully and longingly drawn to an unavailable man, know that your androphobia is at work!

COMPARTMENTALIZING RELATIONSHIPS WITH MEN

Many androphobic women do form a relationship with an available man and even get married, but they're unwilling or unable to let him become an integrated part of their lives, fiercely guarding their independence. You think of him as demanding, as a central focus that detracts from your other interests, not understanding that he can be part of the whole fabric of your life and not distract you from your own growth and experiences.

You keep wanting to compartmentalize him, to keep him in his proper slot, and if he resists being so contained, you automatically see him in dangerous competition with the other aspects of your life. For our patient Jackie it was Stan versus her private space, or Stan versus her women friends, or Stan versus the article she was writing. Stan hovered there, threatening to take over everything. Jackie couldn't imagine him integrated into the whole of her life, an enhancement rather than a threat to her separate identity.

She had grown up in a home where her father was away on business trips much of the time. She and her mother missed him a great deal, but in the end developed an unconscious conspiracy to reject this man who disappointed them by his absence. By containing or isolating him, he could no longer hurt them. Today, if Jackie's father walks into a room where she and her mother are talking, it's a conversation stopper. They deal with him briefly and get back to their real concerns, which don't include him.

In some ways the women's movement has fostered the erroneous belief that for a woman independence means independence from a man. But this form of liberation in fact supports the old-fashioned notion that male capacities are limited. You relegate men to a narrow space in your personal life when you have a vivid image of your father only washing the car, doing the lawn work or handling the finances. He stays in his proper place: the garage, the basement, a particular chair. One sad father said, "Do you know who I am at home? Mr. Checkbook!" His children communicated with him only when they needed money. We hear similar expressions of hurt from single men who are arbitrarily shut out from sharing a central role in the lives of the women they are seeing.

Androphobic women don't know that closeness with a man can support rather than detract from their autonomy. They believe they have to drop everything when a man presents himself. They have no female role model whose husband is part of her deepest concerns, who lightens her burdens so she can do her own work better, whose loving support energizes her toward greater creativity and productivity. As long as they isolate men, they'll never find out what their presence could do for them. The feminist claim "What I really need is a wife" is absolutely true. For a woman, "wife" is a husband—the kind her mother may never have had.

In the company of a less servile and more self-actualized woman, a man will share the joys of her accomplishments. Instead of compartmentalization, there is a free flow of contact with the man as involved and interested in her activities as she is in his. They share and participate in one another's doings. The man can move closer or back off, but he doesn't have to disappear entirely for the woman to be able to think about herself.

When Phyllis was drawing up a proposal for a book she wanted to write, she told her boyfriend not to call her for two weeks so she could give her project her undivided attention. Henry was hurt that she felt his presence as a bother, particularly because he was very supportive of her.

If you are an androphobic woman, a man is an irritant. You haven't experienced getting much loving support, so you're uncomfortable with it. Your self-sufficiency makes it difficult for you to gracefully receive the nurturing, the comfort and the help of a partner. When you need it the most, you habitually push it away.

Your personal history has implanted in you the belief that men are hard to deal with. As a result, you feel you need always to control a man. You allow him certain days or evenings, restricting his activities, even isolating him when you most need a partner. Only when you risk giving up control and allow a free flow will you discover what a husband can mean to you.

·11·
REJECTING THE LOVE
YOU NEED

The tragic result of androphobia is that you can develop such strong defenses to protect yourself from pain that you push away the loving relationship you most need. When you are harboring feelings of hurt or betrayal from the past, it can be an automatic response to become suspicious and angry when a man sincerely offers love to you. Instead of being receptive, you become cold, or put his love to an impossible test. On a deep level, you have locked yourself up and thrown away the key.

In our therapy with androphobic women, it is very important to help them understand the dynamic of rejecting love when it is available, in spite of wanting and needing it. They might overcome their fears enough to allow a close relationship to develop, but then feel a strong urge to reject the very man they love.

Defensive Rejection
•

We have discovered a primitive defense mechanism used by androphobic women to keep themselves from admitting they want love. It's called defensive rejection.

Georgina was plagued by the fact that she didn't feel love for her mother. A teacher, she was experienced as a loving and generous person by her colleagues and students. But whenever Georgina thought of her mother, a cold and distant feeling came over her; she couldn't feel the warmth for her mother that she felt toward most people. Georgina's mother complained that she didn't visit more often, so her guilty daughter occasionally took the train home bringing little gifts and samples of school projects, hoping to patch up their relationship.

On one such trip, Georgina fought off edgy nervousness all the way, remembering her intention to have only good feelings for her mother. After all, she couldn't think of anything "bad" that her mother had ever done to her. That afternoon she was at the kitchen table having tea with her mother. Whenever she spoke, she saw an evasive, uncomfortable look come across her mother's face. It seemed like her mother didn't grasp anything Georgina was saying. When Georgina brought out some teaching materials to show her, her mother changed the subject. When she gave her mother the gifts she'd brought, the response was detached and dismissive. Suddenly a clear thought went through Georgina's mind: "My mother doesn't love me." Instantly she felt the familiar coldness come over her. Her face became grim, her jaws tightened.

Georgina was experiencing the primitive defense of

young children faced with an unloving parent. If we had to put the defense into words, it would be "If you don't love me, then I won't love you." This defiant, seemingly strong position isn't as prideful as it seems. It's a desperate tactic, because a child needs love for her very survival. The response is essentially a dare, a poignant challenge from a vulnerable child who can't really afford to adopt the loveless stance she learns to mimic in response to an unloving parent. Not feeling love for her mother is a primitive attempt to force her mother to love her.

Androphobic women are locked into this loving yet hating stand-off position with someone important in their lives. "Since you don't love me, I won't love you back." On a superficial level that might sound like a healthy, self-respecting response. The problem is that defensive rejection is irrational and total. It implies that a crime has been committed, and nothing can assuage the pain. Trust has been violated, the deed is done, the gates shut down forever. Love cannot penetrate this living prison. This spiteful, immature posture can be maintained throughout life by those who reject love and refuse to give it. It's a case of cutting off your nose to spite your face. That's why an androphobic woman is so needy—by employing defensive rejection in one or more significant early relationships, she develops a reserved, withholding position with most other people as well. In her needy condition she is so sensitive to rejection that she will no longer reach out to show her need, foreseeing only hurt if she makes herself vulnerable again. She sees everything through this distorted lens. Of course, her defense is fully understandable, but the longer it lasts the less useful it is to her. She has locked herself into a loveless script.

When a woman says, "I never share my feelings openly with anyone," or when she makes a (characteristically) cynical remark—"Wouldn't you just know he'd pick the day of my birthday to have an asthma attack!"—we are alerted to her stance of defensive rejection. You've probably witnessed cases of defensive rejection in families. A friend told us of her two aunts who live across the street from each other in a midwestern town, but haven't spoken in twenty years. There are parents who cut off beloved children from inheritances, and those who have never said "I love you" to them. Feeling hurt and rejected themselves as children, they feel justified in freezing someone out.

Defensive rejection occurs whenever someone refuses to speak and creates a silent stand-off, which is really a disguised invitation to be pursued. The trouble starts when you begin to believe your own aloof act. You forget that you need love, that your icy demeanor is a childish dare to others to try to win your love. This pattern of not relating is passed on in families when an unloved woman creates the same stand-off with her children, and they in turn reject their own.

Georgina learned defensive rejection from her mother, and later discovered a pattern of being easily insulted in her relationships with men. There was always a point when a man "did something" and Georgina would turn to ice, losing perspective on the trivial nature of the "crime," comfortably locking herself into her stand-off position. She was able to unravel this compulsive defense in therapy—a defense against her own vulnerability and fear of intimacy—when she finally admitted that she truly did love her mother, despite her mother's weaknesses and hurtful behaviors, and that she was simply protecting herself by withdrawing from her. She also discovered that she had loved certain men in the past whom she had also compulsively rejected.

The guarded woman becomes depressed and stroke-starved—that's the main problem with defensive rejection. Dares don't really work. A woman with an uptight readiness to be hurt drives men away. She may say she wants to be courted, but it's a case of the Taming of the Shrew: She wants a man to bring forth her love *in spite of* her cynicism and emotional detachment.

To become available for the satisfying level of intimacy you need, you must admit the deep desire for love that is behind your defenses. Even men you "despised" have incurred your negative feelings because of the love you wanted from them—the degree of hatred they engendered being barometers of your neediness and readiness to give them all your love. Even if you feel an icy distance from your parents, your inner child really wants to love them. It's because they either rejected, hurt or exploited you in some way that you are protecting yourself from them now. You once needed love from the very people who have disappointed you, and admitting this will help remove a barrier that keeps love out of your life.

The Turandot Effect: Testing a Man

Puccini's opera *Turandot* is the story of a deeply androphobic woman, a woman needing love yet resisting all suitors.

Turandot is a young woman whose tragic inheritance of a loveless script from the past keeps her a victim. She is deeply influenced by the plight of an ancient ancestress who once loved and trusted a foreigner who then betrayed her by conquering her city and carrying her into exile, where she died of grief.

To avenge her ancestral princess, the seemingly strong Turandot insists that any man who wants to marry her submit to a test that consists of answering three riddles. If he fails, the penalty is death. She is famous for her beauty, so many men do court her, but all fail the tests and all are executed—except Calaf.

Turandot asks Calaf, "What is the phantom that is born by night and dies every day?" He answers, "It is what now inspires me, Hope."

"What is it that is like a fever, yet grows cold when you die? It blazes up when you think of great deeds?" He answers, again correctly, "The blood."

The last question she asks is, "What is the ice that sets you on fire?" After some time he answers, "You are the ice that sets me on fire, Turandot."

Turandot becomes frightened when Calaf answers all the riddles correctly. She begs the emperor not to give her over to Calaf as a slave, because Calaf is a foreigner. She fears the plight of her ancestress.

Later, when Calaf is alone with Turandot, he accuses her of cruelty but then kisses her passionately. Suddenly, her lifelong fierceness and need for revenge are gone. Trumpets blare and Turandot announces to the court, "I have discovered the stranger's secret, and his name is Love."

The androphobic woman tends to put a man to the

test, particularly one who gets close to her. We call this the Turandot Effect. She may relate to him with puzzling behavior that confuses him as to what she wants. She is so ambivalent he feels "damned if he does and damned if he doesn't." She compulsively needs to test him, and seems to *want* him to fail. She feels such desperation in relating to him that she wants to "kill him" if he can't solve her problems.

Essentially, Turandot's riddles represent her psychological problems. The first is despair. She is tortured by her lack of trust and inability to feel love. At night, in fantasy, she feels hope, but it disappears by day in the face of reality: Men fail her and incur her rage. Calaf has the answer. He understands her lack of hope, and offers her his own.

Turandot's second problem concerns passion. She is filled with repressed love. In identifying "the blood," or passion, Calaf shows he understands these feelings and accepts them in her, opening the way for self-acceptance and expression of passionate feelings.

She also secretly cries out to be rescued from her loneliness. She demands that Calaf love her in spite of her coldness. "You are the ice that sets me on fire," he tells her.

The trouble for real-life Turandots is that there aren't many Calafs around. When a war of trust is going on in a woman's mind, she is so vulnerable that she doesn't know whether to resist the love she needs or accept it. That's why she gives a man such a confusing, hard time.

The Turandot Effect is a symptomatic response when an androphobic woman starts loving someone. Fear is expressed through panic and highly irrational behavior.

Steve has had many years of firsthand experience dealing with the Turandot Effect. He has weathered critical man-testing sessions with androphobic patients who are filled with a suspicious kind of hatred just when they are beginning to trust. They suddenly find fault with the therapist—not being brilliant enough, not being available by phone at a particular moment, seeming to be more friendly with a previous patient.

Gwen, a single young woman, was the daughter of an alcoholic father and had never felt close to a man. Lonely and depressed, she didn't know how to break out of the pattern of lovelessness. She came to therapy twice a week, and after several months began to develop a positive connection to Steve. It was a healing relationship in which she was able to discuss many aspects of her life, receiving advice and encouragement to discover her own strengths.

At a certain point, it was time for her to change her basic beliefs about men, based upon the positive experience she was having with Steve. That's when her fear came out. She began feeling an incredible surge of anxiety as the time of her appointments drew near. Her heart beat faster and her blood pressure rose. She arrived at therapy sessions feeling distressed, even panicked, and felt great relief when the sessions were over. Looking back on those months, Gwen said later, "Those sessions meant everything in the world to me, and yet it was the worst ordeal of the week."

If it is difficult for a therapist to weather the storms of the Turandot Effect, you must realize it's even harder for an ordinary, well-meaning guy who cares about you but hasn't a clue as to what's happening. A therapist's function includes receiving and analyzing the anger aroused when a woman's defenses begin to crumble, but it's too much to expect a man to love you no matter how much you reject and criticize him. If you have severe androphobia, you may need professional help. Therapists are trained to understand the dynamics of unconscious fear, and the sometimes hostile defenses used to ward it off when it begins to surface. A therapist knows how to hang in there with you and to interpret your fears. You'll learn how to stop acting them out in ways that sabotage your very goal of opening up to love.

No man is a Calaf, but some can help you better than others. There are men who can love a woman deeply, but are completely unable to negotiate the manifestations of her neurosis. In the opera, many lovers had failed Turandot because they were naive about her problems (riddles). You might be rejecting true love just because a man doesn't have the savvy to get around your defenses. It's important therefore to take responsibility for the fear reactions that love causes you and get the help you need in learning to trust.

Letting Love Win

One of the major psychological problems of our times is that many people are emotionally numb and fear their deep feelings. In many single people, the sense of loss inspired by divorce or relationships that didn't work often feels overwhelming. This may be why it has even become stylish to "stay cool." Thus we expect to achieve intimacy in sex without love being present, expect to suffer breakups without jealousy or bitterness and have serious relationships without passionate attachment. And whenever the pain of intense emotion threatens, some people escape to drugs, frenetic social activity and overwork. But a primary part of overcoming your psychological resistance to loving a man is to *let yourself begin to feel*—even if it hurts.

You may first need a therapeutic relationship in which you have enough support that you let yourself experience your deepest feelings. You must open up the past in order to put it behind you. You must cry your tears, paving the way for emotional acceptance. And finally, you must take responsibility for being afraid. It is *you* who has reacted with fear. It is *you* who burdens present relationships with your past experiences. Taking responsibility is not a guilt trip on yourself, but the way to cease being a victim. That's how you outgrow your fear of love.

Here is a list of some of the points you should be concerned with in your goal of letting love win out in your life:

1. Be aware if you are quick to get insulted and withdraw from relationships. The habit of defensive rejection will keep you from getting close to a partner.

2. The next time someone upsets you, tell that person you're feeling hurt. Learn to reach out instead of retreating in times of need.

3. If you feel chronically disappointed by men, judgmental and critical of them, you must work through your problems in trusting an intimate.

4. Stop expecting perfect sensitivity from men and feeling insulted when they fail to come through. In a spirit of acceptance and good humor, expect to teach a man how to give you what you need.

5. Don't blame a man for your past disappointments.

Therapy is a better place to explore your pain than courtship.

6. Take responsibility for the emotional baggage you bring into a relationship. Your problems are *not* an excuse for treating a man disrespectfully. When you are upset with him, you may be tempted to release anger from the past. Restrain yourself from this destructive behavior.

7. Realize that if you were rejected in childhood, you will have a tendency to reject others. Fight this tendency by reaching out. This isn't so hard if you stay honest about your need for closeness. When you push others away, you're pretending that you're not lonely and that you don't need love.

8. Develop a positive image of a relationship that is not a trap. Picture the future with a man you are dating as full of adventures and new opportunities. Constricting relationships are always frightening.

9. Understand that past disappointments may irrationally intrude on the present when you start to get close. This doesn't mean it's time to break up, but that there are problems to be solved. Seek out counseling if you have trouble resolving these issues.

10. Know that love is vital to an emotionally satisfying life. Look for a nice guy with whom you can overcome your fears of love.

What Men Fear in Relationships

Once you begin to understand your own hidden fears and overcome the resistance to love they cause, you will be much more open to loving a man. The next step will be to learn to deal with some of *his* fears. Focusing on a man's fears will actually help you finish overcoming your own because you will feel equal to and as powerful as the man you love. As you reach out to respond to his fears, you will be appreciative of how far you have come yourself.

A man's resistance is not exactly the same as yours, although a woman who places a high premium on independence can identify with some of these male dynamics. Women usually are not centrally important to men. Integrity, power and selfhood tend to take center stage in men's lives. Male fears have more to do with loss of self than loss of love, and they mistrust anything that makes them feel vulnerable and weak.

THE FEAR OF LOSING POWER

A sense of his power is vital to a man. Most men have a strong image of what it means to be a man, and this vision of masculinity drives them to be successful. But it also makes them fearful inside. Since their focus is on maintaining power in interactions with others, it is strategic that only the strong parts of their personalities be revealed. This is why men fear situations in which their feelings are exposed.

As a result, men fear their feelings. They don't particularly want to experience them, and they certainly don't want to discover any pockets of weakness within themselves. As we discussed earlier, when a man tries to stay invulnerable, he sacrifices depth relationships, looking to sex alone to supply his emotional needs for closeness.

It is important for a woman to acknowledge the passionate attachment a man can have to the masculine ego ideal. On this issue, he must be carefully understood, because he will be especially self-protective to cover his fears. But he needs to learn that there also can be strength in intimate sharing, and in a relinquishing of male posturing.

We are aware of the terrible toll of stress this unfeeling stance takes on men. Death by heart attack is an extreme but all too common example of an implosion of unexpressed emotions. Researchers in Type A behavior claim that heart attacks result partly from emotional repression. These experts are finding that the expression of emotions—love, neediness, even grief— help dissipate the tension and irritable temper that characterize a heart attack-prone individual.

THE FEAR OF BEING TRAPPED

The classic male fear of marriage is the fear of being trapped. A man has a childhood developmental pattern in which he finds his identity when he rejects his attachment to the female, his mother, and joins the world of men. And his main example of how to be a man may have been an emotionally distant father who was more involved with his job than with his family.

Thus, his early conditioning causes a man to view domestic life as a trap. A self-respecting man does not want to spend his days feeling imprisoned. He is happy that he got away from home. Why should he want another one?

Eric expressed it well. "I call it the velvet trap," he said. "Here I am with this sweet, beautiful woman. She is lovely, in her cashmere sweater with pearls and delicate perfume. Her body is voluptuous and she wants love, sex and babies. Lots of babies!

"She wants to marry me and get out of the city, live in a sweet house with roses over the door. Why would I want to do that? I love the city, and I hate the suburbs and commuting. Do I want to spend my life on the train, working to buy the house, paying for her to have the pleasure of babies, and their college educations? Of course I don't. But when I am next to that cashmere sweater and she is so sweet, it scares me. I have to admit that her love means a lot to me, but I don't want to get caught in the velvet trap!"

Men value their independence, fearing both dependence on someone and having someone be dependent upon them. They fear a narrow life in which they will miss out on adventures. The thought of increasing financial burdens is frightening. This prospect of not making enough money can be the worst fear of all. The only way for you to help a man with his fear of entrapment is to develop a relationship that will not be a trap for him—or you either.

The best relationships are ones that make you feel free. Eric is now married, but to a different woman than the one he was describing. His new wife has her own profession, and they are equal breadwinners. They live in a co-op in the city, and he has neither given up his squash games nor his penchant for dining out. Life is even more exciting than in his bachelor days. He and his wife are expecting their first, and probably only, child. Marriage is not a trap when the benefits clearly outweigh the sacrifices.

THE FEAR OF ABANDONMENT

In the past men were very well defended against experiencing their abandonment anxiety because of what we call the Pumpkin Eater syndrome. Women were kept at home and men never considered that their wives could live without them. Where would women go? How could they support themselves? If a wife occasionally flirted with a job opportunity, or more daringly, with another man, the husband of twenty or more years ago might briefly feel his own abandonment anxiety. A few noisy threats usually took care of the matter, and the husband could again be comfortable in the knowledge that women need men, not vice versa.

Times have changed, and the new independent woman is putting the level of male abandonment anxiety, as well as male performance anxiety, at an all-time high. A man might feel that she really should be back in her dependent place in order for his fears to go away, but he cannot make the clock go backward. Better to avoid these threatening creatures altogether is one solution. Others dare to involve themselves with women who seem not to need them as much, because they can pay their own way.

A man can get in touch with his own needs for a woman when she is resourceful and shows that she has a life that is independent from him. This perception can arouse his fear that she might someday leave him. "It's about time," you might say to yourself. "Give him a dose of his own medicine. Let *him* feel the abandonment anxiety we women have suffered these many eons." But men are not very good with pain. They fear it as they do all emotions that make them feel weak. When a man fears abandonment, he (like you) needs reassurance, and lots of it.

It's a good idea to help a man save face when he's suffering abandonment anxiety. In this vulnerable state he knows he needs you, and he'll be forever grateful to you for helping him out. You can let him know you will miss him deeply when you are on that fabulous business trip to Tokyo. You can tell him that the week at the spa would have been much better with him there. Many times we have seen a woman blow it just when her love would really count, perhaps in retaliation for all the times in the past when her love or need was discounted. She builds up resentment against her man when he acts super strong, so she is tempted to tease him when he is vulnerable, rather than help and comfort him.

The mistake women make is in actually buying the strong man act. It is important to realize that every man is terribly vulnerable to abandonment when he cares about a woman. If you are seeing a divorced man who is extremely marriage-shy, you must be aware of his abandonment issues. Many men are being left by women these days. Be aware of how you might scare the daylights out of the man in your life by saying "I think I might like to relocate to another city one of these days." Do *not* play games with his fears by implying that you don't need him, or he will defensively retreat from you. When you have the edge, use it to strengthen the love you share rather than hitting below the belt. This is a golden opportunity for you to show him that feelings of weakness are opportunities for receiving comfort. When he is aware that he needs you, he should learn to reach out for your comfort; this teaches him to relinquish macho defenses and count on you.

TRIGGER POINTS

In every relationship you will eventually have to deal with problems of the other person as well as your own. These are the trigger points that threaten to distance you from one another. Frankly, problems are a big turn-off in a relationship. You can be on the way to getting very close, close enough to consider marriage, and suddenly you are forced to deal with a very unpleasant aspect of a person's psychological makeup.

It is one thing to deal with your own problems with intimacy. But when the tables are turned you are an accused, innocent bystander. Your man, like a Turandot, is choosing you with whom to recreate some unpleasant issue of his past life. "Who needs this?" you might ask yourself. Your partner's behavior seems bizarre. As Rebecca so bluntly put it, "The closer we get, the more crap we have to deal with."

An even worse, but common, scenario is when one person's problems bring out those of the other person. This could be called a case of interlocking scripts. Both lovers suddenly start treating one another horribly, and yet are very confused because they really do love each other. This is not pathological! It happens to anybody who has problems from the past that they have not resolved—and this means pretty much everybody. Getting close triggers a compulsion to work out your problems with your partner.

The goal here is to get a psychological problem to lose its power over the present situation. As a partner, you must learn how to help your mate get some perspective. All good partners are therapists to one another, but they need to be more direct than a professional therapist would be. Instead of wringing your hands, try to get to the bottom of things. Even the most wonderful partners will be tempted to enact some problematic drama with you. Once you have searched your own conscience, make it clear that you are not the problem, but that you have sympathy for the unpleasant feelings the other person is experiencing.

Pat was dating a man whose mother talked too much and too loudly. In restaurants he started hushing her whenever she spoke with excitement or animation. This infuriated her, and after some psychological detective work she figured out his problem. She expressed sympathy, but firmly stated that she was being normally expressive, was not his mother and was not to be shushed! The inappropriate behavior stopped, and they went on with their courtship.

Audrey became suspiciously irate whenever her fiancé would hug her in the kitchen. They often cooked and cleaned up together, and he would embrace her as she rinsed the dishes or tossed the salad. It turned out that she had done too many dishes as a kid, and she thought that somehow he was rewarding her with affection for her domestic contributions. Her bitchiness was an overdue statement to her parents that she did not want kitchen duty anymore. These are minor psychological problems that could destroy wonderful relationships if they are not squarely addressed.

Sometimes you become annoyed or befuddled by problems your very presence seems to stimulate in your partner. Or, in reverse, you experience your own upset but irrational feelings and figure that he mysteriously caused these negative reactions. Unfortunately, getting close stimulates an unfair projection of unresolved issues for most of us. This seemingly hopeless situation happens to everyone.

Couples who make it have learned how to go the distance in spite of inevitable problems. This means keeping perspective and knowing that exaggerated emotional reactions probably have little to do with the present situation. Once the feeling is placed historically where it belongs, it can lose its power. This is one of the miracles of psychological insight. Sometimes an issue seems trivial when put in historical perspective, but even if it is very serious, you must make it clear that although you may *trigger* negative feelings, you did not *cause* them. A creative process can develop in which you each agree to take responsibility for strong feelings and trace them to their source. Some trigger points we have observed are these:

- Men whose intrusive mothers bossed them around too much can be set off by a simple request.
- Women who did too much housekeeping and caretaking as children get set off by domestic work.
- Men who were not allowed to have feelings of vulnerability or to ask for what they wanted get angry when their mates cannot read their minds.
- Women whose mothers or fathers were very crit-

ical of them can feel tortured by just a furled brow.
- Men or women who had too little spending money as children get feelings of hopeless deprivation if they must curtail their spending.
- Men or women who did not have enough fun as children react with irrational anger if their mate wants to leave the party early.
- Men whose mothers were depressed are overwhelmed by female tears.
- Women whose fathers were undemonstrative consider the lack of a valentine an unforgivable offense.

Because all human relationships are imperfect, it's likely that a prospective partner will have problems from the past that he will bring to your relationship, as will you. You'll inevitably push a button that will elicit an unexpectedly intense response. The most important principle to follow is this: Problems exist to be solved. Although negative emotions can be very upsetting, the problems they reflect may be minor once they are made conscious and worked through.

In coaching many men and women through this process, we've often heard an interesting piece of feedback: "If I had known how to do this, I probably would have worked things out in a previous relationship."

·12·
LOVE LEADS TO MARRIAGE

In a recent interview the Metropolitan Opera soprano Eva Marton explained her signature interpretation of Turandot: "She is afraid of surrendering herself to any would-be prince, but she fancies finding one." Once you understand your fear response, you can move toward the other side of your conflicting emotions, your desire to love a man and to marry him.

Loving Yourself First

You must be able to love yourself before you can have a relationship that will lead to a satisfying marriage. Loving yourself helps you work through any hidden fears that trouble you. When you truly love yourself, you will never be lonely again with or without a man to love—you will have yourself. A woman who likes herself has more to give in a relationship. Her self-esteem makes her attractive, whereas a woman who doesn't like herself is automatically in a neurotic stance with respect to other people.

An insecure person can't be intimate or generous, but instead plays games to compensate for her lack of self-acceptance. Interestingly, too, if you don't like yourself, the people you really want to be with will be annoyed by signs of your self-hate. You can put no greater burden on another person than a lack of self-love, because no one can really help you with this problem. People lacking in self-esteem destroy relationships by manipulating the emotions of others. Taking too much, they persistently feel that the generosity of their friends is never enough.

Frances describes her problems with men in this way: "There seem to be two types of men out there, the older, strong, married kind and the weak, needy, loser men." She doesn't realize that her own unresolved issues of self-hate polarize all men into rescuers or fellow victims. The relationships Frances forms are unstable and soon break down. It's a terrible experience, compounding her deep-seated belief that something is wrong with her. There is simply no substitute for loving yourself, taking good care of yourself and developing your own grounded identity.

Few of us are blessed with adequate self-love. The origins of one's self-esteem are in the reflected, loving appraisal of others: family, friends, colleagues. Whatever loving mirrors were lacking in childhood, there comes a time in everyone's life to assume responsibility for one's own self-acceptance. The following suggestions can help you in developing greater self-love:

- Take good mental and physical care of yourself. Realizing that you are on your own, assume responsibility for being your own caregiver.
- Have a lot of people in your life. Let different people give to you in different ways. Enjoy both the giving and receiving of strokes from your various friends.
- Accomplish things, and count your accomplishments. From the time you enter school through adult life, a major source of self-esteem comes from the work you do.
- Cultivate satisfying, enriching pastimes. The list is endless, including sports, reading, art, music, gardening, theater and travel.
- Think positively about your assets, options and possibilities.
- Fight your tendencies to be negative. Don't commiserate with others or wallow in self-pity about your inadequacies.
- Cultivate impeccable habits of personal grooming. You are responsible for feeling strong, vital and attractive. When you care for your body, you are performing an act of self-love.
- Create the right living environment for yourself, being aware of your needs for comfort and beauty.
- Develop your talents, not just for work, but for pleasurable fulfillment. Keep growing—artistically, mentally or socially—and get better at what you do well.
- Nurture the spiritual dimension in your life, appreciating your roots and your values. Participate in the sublime levels of life through music, art, literature, even humor.

- Stay in a positive and optimistic place in regard to other people, appreciating their assets and possibilities. Because of human interdependence, negativity toward others always reflects back upon the self. Instead, be a generous (but not martyred) giver to others.
- Pay attention to your thoughts and feelings, and tell your own truth. Say yes when you mean it and no when you need to.

If you find yourself deficient in any of these aspects of self-care, you may not have enough self-love. Healthy self-esteem is a precondition to forming a healthy bond with any man.

UNCONDITIONAL LOVE

True self-acceptance is unconditional. Of course you appreciate your accomplishments, but they aren't the reasons why you love yourself. Unconditional self-love means loving yourself the way you were born, not having to prove anything. Your temperament, talents, personality and history are the things you can't change no matter what. Learn to love yourself on that deep level, simply for who you are. For a single woman, this means loving yourself without being married. You are okay as a person without marriage, and if you never find Mr. Right, you are still okay.

When you achieve this freedom of self-acceptance, something happens that enhances your chance of getting married, if that's what you want. Sally said, "When I gave up trying so hard, it miraculously came my way."

The principle involved here is not giving up on marriage, but giving up on marriage as a cure for damaged self-esteem. This means forgetting your obsession with finding a man who can make you feel good about yourself.

It isn't a mystery why acceptance of yourself as unmarried can lead to marriage. You've removed a formidable pressure from both yourself and the man you meet. In addition, unconditional self-love means that you'll be authentic, and therefore available to be contacted as a person, with all your interesting quirks. When you try too hard to be impressive you usually don't reveal the natural qualities that your friends love about you. You should accept your idiosyncrasies and not hide them in the interest of people-pleasing. This attitude invites positive energy. By developing positive inner attitudes, you create the right magnetic field around you to draw love in your direction.

EXPRESSING THE FEMININE

Love is generally considered a "feminine" emotion, and when men allow themselves to love, they activate the feminine part of their psyches. In other words, they become more emotionally expressive, empathic, nurturing and generous.

During the relationship revolution some of these qualities were dismissed by women. We can understand why women would relinquish the feminine dimension: They needed to organize themselves more traditionally, as men have, becoming focused on tasks and more goal-oriented. But when women stop loving, they're in trouble. Their good reason for rejecting the traditional task of tending the hearth was that this role damaged their self-esteem. Loving was not appreciated as valuable work, and even made them vulnerable to abuse. But it's time now for you to consider again the kind of caring that makes relationships work. Self-love means operating with a sense of your own power, but it also means appreciating the value of the traditionally female perspective, which is to show men the value of empathy and caring for others.

Discovering Your Love for Men

Many women who are afraid of men behave as though they have something against them. An androphobic woman must open herself to positive feelings about the male gender. Men are people, too. In our times and in this culture men can be different from women in ways that may seem unattractive to you. They project more aggressive energy and exhibit more self-centeredness. They may show less emotional feeling than you would like, seeming deficient in tenderness and sensitivity. At least that's what seems to be true on the outside.

But differences don't have to be feared. In fact, they can be fascinating as points of contact leading to mutual stimulation and growth. Instead of being fearful of men, learn to enjoy them *because* of their differences.

Women today are having difficulty finding mates because of rising expectations coupled with naiveté about men. They refuse to deal with men as they really are. They demand that men change according to the principles of feminism, which galvanized a powerful sense of entitlement. Fueled by their outrage at women's historical victimization in the home, they insist today on finding husbands who will understand them emotionally, fulfill them sexually (with regular experiences of ecstasy) and who will be deeply supportive of whatever interests them. A modern woman bases her profile of an acceptable man on a fantasy of what she believes she deserves, and in so doing has eliminated most of the men alive as possible love prospects.

There is nothing wrong with wanting a satisfying relationship, but the expected terms of satisfaction are often extreme. Beware of holding up an impossible ideal that sounds more like the combination of a perfect mother and father than like an actual garden-variety man.

TAKING MEN OFF THEIR PEDESTALS

For a woman who fears men, detaching from her unrealistic expectations of them addresses only half of the problem. It's not only unrealistic expectations about men that creates her problems in loving them, but also naiveté. You may be surprised that we call today's single woman "naive" about men. After all, she is liberated and sophisticated. She may have been married previously, may either have lived with a man or had a serious love affair. She probably has had several sexual partners, and may spend her working life in the center of the male business world. The kind of naiveté we are referring to, however, is the sort we see in our single patients and it's characterized by an undue awe of men.

Androphobic women typically describe men in images that are larger than life.

Estelle's boss was a "fantastic leader of men with an iron will." Jo Ann talked of having lunch with a "gorgeous man with a stupendous intellect." Pat described a man at work who was "so smooth and manipulative, he could get anybody to do anything."

When androphobic women speak of men with such hyperbole, their seeming praise conceals a hidden fear. If you are scared and threatened by a man, he will seem to be inordinately powerful. Ask yourself if you tend to put a man on a pedestal, and then to tremble in awe of him.

The phenomenon of awe always involves fear. The androphobic woman doesn't see men clearly, as ordinary mortals. Just as unrealistic expectations keep her from forgiving a typically imperfect male, her sense of awe about a man's specialness is also unrealistic. The greatness or fearsomeness she describes is a figment of her imagination. Men gladly contribute to the hype, because they like to act larger than life. But it takes an androphobic woman to go along with the image the puffed-up male wants to project. Ironically, however, an especially power-hungry man often feels frustrated because he has surrounded himself with awestruck followers who cannot really love him. Feeling awe is never a mature expression of love, because the involvement is between unequal persons, one weaker than the other— perhaps not intrinsically weaker, but because the awestruck person has given away his or her own power.

A woman who loves a man in a mature way feels strong about herself and sees him in true perspective, loving him for his genuine self. Loving has to do with appreciating the ordinary, human qualities of another person. Such love is unconditional, not reflecting accomplishments so much as intrinsic qualities. A woman without undue fears of a man will see him as mortal no matter how impressive his accomplishments or extreme his grandiosity. She describes him without exaggeration as kind, fun, friendly or smart. Men are neither gods nor devils.

THE AWESOME MEN IN YOUR PAST

It's important to accept how the men in your past inspired fear in you. You must appreciate that the impact of a grown man, your father, upon you occurred at a time when you were most susceptible to experiencing awe: when you were a little girl. Men can seem gruff and upsetting to other adults, so imagine their effect on children, who take everything to heart. Imagine how difficult moments were filtered through your child's mind, severely testing your coping resources.

A little girl sees men through a magnifying glass, and that image gets fixed in her mind. As an adult, she will tend to repeat this magnifying process. Adele, who had an unusually cruel father, experiences her boss as a giant. When he walks past her desk casually, she feels a large, foreboding, hovering presence. He's actually a very low-key guy, and other people aren't spooked by him at all.

The way to stop magnifying men is to come to terms with the men in your past. Learn to accept them as ordinary people. The goal is not to condone their problems, but to understand and accept them. If you can do this, you will be doing yourself a big favor. In effect you are saying, "I am big enough to look at my father as a real person." Look with objectivity, focusing on his background, what influenced him as you were growing up and the stresses in his life that may have resulted in his adopting awe-inspiring behavior. You're on your way to curing your androphobia when you demystify men and thus take the awe out of your experiences with them.

LOOKING FOR AFFECTION

Sometimes childhood awe is based on a history of being neglected by your father. Edith told of her minister who patted her on the arm as she left church each Sunday, and of how she was overwhelmed by the experience of his affection, which she had never received at home. Holly talked about her feelings for her girlfriends' fathers. She worshipped them and thought they were extremely powerful and glamorous. Her own parents were divorced, and she rarely saw her own father.

Encourage yourself to see men as ordinary and human, with both strengths and weaknesses. Shed the magnifying glass of childhood and experience men as they really are. When you develop a realistic view of men, you'll feel comfortable with them and you'll be able to allow loving feelings to emerge. You'll be able to love your man for his human qualities, his frailties and his idiosyncrasies. You'll sense the reality of who he is. The upsurge of genuine affection and love that you'll feel has nothing to do with his being chairman of the board, or with his buying you candy and flowers, or doing anything traditionally "romantic." You'll look at him without demanding that he change or *do* anything.

The Myth of Mr. Right

When you are ready for love, you will give up unrealistic fantasies and find a real man to care for. Stop looking for Prince Charming, the sugar daddy with a fat bank account—or even the perfectly enlightened feminist male. These are all unrealistic projections of a woman's fantasies and they bear little relationship to real life in marriage. Get in touch with your particular fantasies about men. They are keeping you from the adventure, the struggle and the joy of the real thing.

The profile of Mr. Right as our single women patients describe him goes something like this: He has pots of money and is impressively good-looking. He can inspire women to love him and to feel deep sexual passion. They won't have to work through any of their own fears, because he'll never do anything to provoke them. In fact, he'll magically fix things emotionally. Since he can practically read a woman's mind, he'll do all the right things—he'll be great at entertaining you, picking wonderful things to do, and will never be at a loss for clever, stimulating conversation. Of course, he has impressive professional and social credentials, and everyone you know will like him very much and be green with envy that you've landed such a catch.

If you're looking for a man who has any of these qualities, look no more. The best you'll get will be some acceptable raw material. The myth of Mr. Right is just that: a fairy tale.

A WOMAN'S INFLUENCE

What you can reasonably hope for is a good-hearted ordinary man who can learn how to please you. Husbands, like wives, are created in good relationships. Fine-tuning adjustments are continually taking place. A woman who's been married for fifteen years might finally have the man she was looking for—a fully developed husband who does the important things right. After all those years, the role of husband is part of his very being. If they've worked out their problems along the way, it will be in his character to care about his wife's feelings and to monitor the effects of his behavior on her.

As a fledgling husband he probably required a lot of attention from his wife to make sure that he saw *her* side of things. She guided him toward thoughtful behaviors, speaking up so that he remembered to keep her needs and views ever on his mind. She once had to work much harder to get him to understand her and care about her than she does now. A wrinkle in her brow conveys the same message today that required an entire weekend screaming match fifteen years ago. Now he knows her issues well. But more important, he is now fully receptive to her and has grown in generosity and the capacity to care.

Every good husband has been taught and probably been changed by a woman's influence over the course of years. Many traditional housewives had fulfilling marriages because the old-fashioned role of hearth-tender and child-rearer also meant being a good husband-trainer. In studying what creates a happy marriage, researchers point to the female partner as the key ingredient. Most husbands don't express their unmet needs or their unhappiness, nor do they instinctively reach out when their wives are unhappy. It's the woman who senses emotional distancing and communicates these perceptions to her partner. She gives the relationship a chance to succeed. It doesn't seem fair that a woman must be the barometer for the state of their relationship and the catalyst for its growth, but that's the truth of it.

As long as you're on an endless search for perfection, you aren't involved in the only process that will get you the love you want—finding an ordinary man who cares for you enough to participate in growing together. As long as you accept reality, you won't mind if the growth is slow, because it will be happening. Every week, month or year you'll love each other more and better. Essentially, Mr. Right is someone you can influence. But if you are hooked on awe, you won't appreciate the man who can be influenced. He'll seem wimpy.

WIMP PHOBIA

Women who are looking for a man who reawakens their childhood feelings of awe will be disappointed by men who don't overwhelm them charismatically. This is what's happened to many career women who've claimed their own power, only to search desperately for men strong enough to stimulate what they think is the desirable female response: being overwhelmed by a powerful male.

Secretly they also want a man to be strong enough to overpower their *fears*, as if some kind of force could conquer them. But if she has what we call wimp phobia, a woman won't be free to love a man as a real human being. Her fears and her naiveté about what love really means keep her bound to the stereotype of a conquering male and a female who submits to his show of power.

SUSAN'S ANDROPHOBIA

About once a year we will have an argument in which Susan feels that Steve is being impossible. Usually he's a supportive, devoted husband who is interested in her concerns, but he can still be quite irrational on those rare occasions when he gets really angry.

After one such blowup, Susan had a heart-to-heart talk with her cousin Linda, who is also a therapist. She admitted to Linda that Steve's temper is usually stress-related and that "Once it's over, he feels okay. But I'm left feeling furiously upset that I can't get him to control himself or apologize. He's not a bully, but at these moments I feel as if he were."

With Linda's encouragement, Susan evaluated her own history with men, especially how she had been in awe of her grandfather, a country doctor and a cattle rancher. If any man could be deemed "larger than life," it was he. Susan's father too had the same impressive charisma. His "John Wayne persona" and decidedly masculine interests focused upon his two sons left Susan shivering with awe on the sidelines of a male-dominated household.

In adult life, when Steve occasionally let a fuse blow,

Susan literally worshipped his temper, clearly a throw-back from responses learned in childhood. She felt diminished and angry at Steve's freedom to blow up. It was as if all of his good qualities evaporated in the wake of his temper. She refused to view this behavior as the normal, healthy response of a man who has accumulated too much stress.

After discussing all of this with her cousin, Susan acknowledged her own androphobic response, but didn't know how to change it. Once she became upset, her well-meaning husband joined the ranks of all the other intimidating men she had known and loved.

Linda asked, "Do you remember the horses at the ranch?"—a reference to their childhood in Nebraska. "Which was your favorite horse?" Clearly it was Penny, a palomino that gave Susan many smooth, fast rides. "Imagine owning a special horse like Penny who gives you a great ride, but there is something tricky about this horse's temperament. He's jumpy in the barn, and occasionally flares up in the corral and knocks out a slat in the fence. But once you mount him, and he's out on the open range, he gives you a great ride. Do you hate this fabulous horse because of a bit of feisty temperament? Maybe his edginess is part of the spirit that gives you such a good ride! Frankly, Susan, I think that you'll feel much better when you understand that Steve is like a really great horse."

The comparison was so unexpected that it quickly got through Susan's androphobic defenses. Susan worked things out by reasoning that the spirit of the male animal may, like Steve's, express itself in an irritable or even angry way at times of stress.

The trouble with androphobia is that it can run rampant. When triggered, it sounds an alarm bell to which the psyche responds as if the whole house were burning down, even if the problem is just a piece of bread smoking in the toaster. Your partner may trigger your androphobic responses, but that's not the signal for you to reject him. You must look beyond your own fears and appreciate your man for both his strengths and his weaknesses.

The Male Pleasure Principle

Most men can give expression to their strong ego drives because they are closely in touch with what gives them pleasure. Men are usually more directly able to please themselves than are women and are relatively guilt-free when it comes to pursuing what they want. A people-pleasing woman is so accustomed to putting others before herself that she hesitates to do things for herself, or finds herself out of touch with her own desires. Not so with most men. They don't hesitate to enjoy their pleasures: watching a baseball game, playing golf, going sailing or lusting after a beautiful woman.

Of course, women do seek personal satisfactions in life, but the pleasure principle is rarely as central to the way they think and behave as it is to a man. The uninhibited pursuit of pleasure makes men seem selfish: "Why do you want us to go to Florida for our vacation?" Ingrid asked her husband. "Because the hotel is right on the golf course," he answered matter-of-factly, irritated at her "silly" question. "But I don't even play golf!" she cried. Following his own desire for gratifi-cation, he assumed they both should go on a golfing trip to Florida. He felt chagrined when he realized his selfishness. "Well, then, where do *you* want to go?" he asked. Ingrid didn't know.

Often a woman feels angry and resentful toward a man for his self-serving mentality, and she will see this as a form of resistance to her. His other interests com-pete with the attention he should be paying to her, she reasons. We believe that the pleasure principle is central to the way men operate, and that you'll be part of a man's life to the extent that you embrace or accept his interests. This doesn't preclude your having interests of your own, some of which he might share and some not. The point is that you must accept a man's orien-tation around self-gratification. You must understand that if you resent this unduly it's probably because of your own attitude of self-sacrifice, or your own unde-veloped sense of pleasure.

The male pleasure principle is one of the things you have going for you early in a relationship. On a super-ficial level, men love women quickly. A man can easily connect with a woman he finds attractive. He'll im-mediately respond, making overtures by looking charm-ing or acting needy. This is where relationships begin, and a woman shouldn't put herself at odds with the male pursuit of pleasure. As the relationship matures, he can learn to consider your needs as well.

A loving courtship gives a woman a chance to make some inroads into a man's self-involved world. Start by believing that his pleasure orientation is not a bad thing. As a potential partner, you intend to join him, which means enjoying sharing his life and the activities that are part of it. His attachments become your attachments, and the extent to which you don't join up will become a problem. Of course he'll be joining your world as well, but the point is that if you want to be part of a man's self-serving world, you must not fight it but enjoy what it has to offer.

There will be parts of his life that you don't like, which is normal. Nevertheless, you shouldn't attack or undermine his attachments, particularly his friends, his children or his family. If he complains about them himself, you would do well to stay neutral, and be the one who exhibits good will. He can criticize his mother, but will resent it if you take such liberties, and might make you the "bad guy" for expressing the negative thoughts he refuses to admit to himself. You'll create a loving bond to the extent that his attachments become your attachments.

Learning to Love Men

If you've been afraid of men for most of your life, you're going to have to change that attitude if you want to marry. Here are some guidelines for developing a positive attitude toward men.

1. Allow men their differences! It's what makes them most lovable and sexy once you accept them.

2. Accept normal male aggression, and don't let a man's forcefulness in expressing himself intimidate you. If necessary, detach yourself and imagine that he just needs to make noise like a fan at a ball game, or a

speaker on a stage. You can teach him to be more gentle, but don't reject him just because he's a rambunctious male.

3. Forget the romantic images of men that you've read in books or seen in the movies. Learn to have a relationship with a real man. It will be less romantic than fantasy and more like having a good pal.

4. Stop worshipping men as a way of dealing with your fear. Work to see that every man is a person, no matter how powerful he may like to act.

5. See the boy in men you know, and make friends with that little kid. This is the way that most andro-phobic women first get close to a man. When they realize that men, too, have vulnerable feelings, their fears begin to diminish.

6. Don't expect most men to be motherly, even though nurturance is what you need. They will be more likely to give you advice and negative feedback to "help" you, because that's how they treat each other. Appreciate what they do have to offer, and understand and accept their limitations.

7. Don't get "hurt" when a man has trouble with thoughtfulness and tenderness. He can only learn this way of behaving with a partner, because it's contrary to the way men operate with each other in competitive situations.

8. Appreciate male "selfishness" as an orientation toward pleasure that would be good for you to learn. It's his pleasure orientation that will make your sex life satisfying and your lifestyle together full of adventures.

9. Learn the difference between loving someone and being "impressed" by them. When you love a man, you

have warm feelings about his personal, human qualities. Being impressed keeps you at a distance, feeling stimulated but somewhat afraid of him.

10. Be willing to take a long time to teach a man the feminine perspective of life. He will learn to enjoy letting go of his power orientation by relaxing, sharing, feeling, dreaming. A woman has wonderful things to teach a man, and they'll be delightful surprises for him.

·13·
REINVENTING THE
INSTITUTION
OF MARRIAGE

Now that you've covered some distance on your journey of overcoming your inner fears, it's time to look at your goal. You want to come to terms with your fear because you want to get married, but it's partly the specter of unhappy marriages that's made you fearful. It's now time to look at the institution of marriage with fresh eyes, to understand that it doesn't have to be oppressive, that couples are finding new ways to be happily married. Marriage doesn't have to be a trap.

Every woman who plans to get married is faced with the question, "How can I be married and still belong to myself?" When you finally answer that question, you've discovered the kind of marriage that will really work for you, and if the marriage supports and enhances you, it will work. Most women need to remember that what they get is as important as what they give.

Being on the receiving end doesn't mean giving in

to the little girl's fantasy of being taken care of by a man, but rather being free to spend a good part of your time as a married person developing your talents. Marriage can be great when you figure out that it actually supports your independence. If you're really loved and cared for, you can go out and do things in the world with a partner's strength behind you. It's what men have traditionally achieved for years—with women's support.

Marriage today is a lifestyle involving two human beings who ideally pursue individual interests. They grow individually in the context of a shared life, lending support but leaving each other responsible for their own fulfillment. Being married takes care of the need for intimate human attachment, but it can't begin to supply the stimulation that's needed for self-development.

The new marriage *can* give you a sense of freedom— if you let each other be responsible for making your own lives work in the world, while giving one another loving encouragement. Then you're both free to go in your own directions with the additional energy that you have when love is behind you. Love frees you from loneliness. There is someone to come home to at the end of every day.

Bonding without Bondage

The important issue for women in marriage is identity. Human fulfillment is based on having a strong sense of who you are, and then living out that image as fully as possible. When you fear men, your good feeling about yourself is at risk. You are afraid of being hurt, and then of feeling demoralized. You are afraid of being financially dependent or trapped by domestic responsibilities. At the heart is a fear of losing yourself emotionally, intellectually, spiritually.

It's fundamental to a happy marriage that you be grounded in your own identity. Don't look to a man to tell you who you are or what you should do with your life. You can't inherit an identity. That's the sad lesson learned by children of accomplished parents, and by women who marry men they think will take care of them.

Developing a solid identity is your own difficult psychological task, and it's largely discovered through the work you do. The closer your work reflects and expresses who you really are, the stronger and happier you'll be. This important aspect of life, a sense of yourself, is something the marriage itself can't give you. In fact, it can be a threat to your identity if you aren't committed to knowing who you are and belonging to yourself. Men are *not* to blame for this. All of us are alone in the sense that no one else can impart an identity to us—we have to find it for ourselves.

MARRIAGES THAT WORK FOR WOMEN

To find a marriage style that works for you, you must know what makes you happy and then press for it. The pleasure principle that motivates men must also be your driving force. By pleasure we mean real joy in living. What makes you feel most vital? If you can answer this question, you know what ingredients are needed for a satisfactory married life. Pursue your own happiness. It will take an impossible pressure off your relationship. The man in your life is neither the answer nor the source—he is your traveling companion.

Domestic chores make great demands on your resources. To live a full life you must give up drudgery for pleasure. Even if the home arts are meaningful to you, pick your priorities and delegate the rest. This means getting cooperation from family members, ordering in dinner, hiring support services and lowering your standards so that if your house is less than perfect, you won't turn into a shrew. Since the important issue in marriage is identity, separate yours from the state of your house—because that's what enslaves a woman! When you get married you must not become your home; you are first and always a person.

If you identify yourself too much with your environment, you'll spend your days serving others. Even if you're a domestic wonder, you'll only achieve mutual respect and equality when you subtract your identity from housework functions. The reason you get more respect for other accomplishments is because nobody else identifies with those functions. Your husband will always care less about housework, simply because he cares more about himself. When you learn to unhook from maintenance activities you'll become the leading lady in the play, not the servant. Liberation in marriage happens when you can be a wife and mother at the same time that you respect yourself as an individual. This is a new step in the feminist revolution: You can both love yourself *and* be married—if you fight your programming to be a servant. If you don't feel like a servant, your husband's expectations of service won't upset you, and you'll be able to confidently and gently teach him another way.

FREEDOM FROM GUILT

The new marriage is between equals who are willing to divide and share responsibilities. The best marriages are good friendships, spiced with sex and romance. A wonderful thing happens in marriage when you stop being each other's servants—you are free to become friends. You come to each other without agendas listing what the other person is supposed to do or not do to please you.

The expectation that you must always please the other person is a great detriment to relationships. Women are as guilty as men of inflicting "please me" expectations on their partners. A man is simply less likely to comply, so a woman becomes the victimized one, angrily blaming her noncompliant husband. You must give up the idea that marriage partners are instruments in the service of each other's happiness.

It's much more exciting to have a friendship between partners who share the pleasures and struggles of life. Intellectual companionship means more than being nursemaid. If two people act like independent adults, they can enjoy intimacy without the burden of caretaking. Of course, there are times when service is appropriate, but it must not be the primary dynamic in a good relationship. Repeat this litany to yourself: "I am his friend, not his cook. I am his friend, not his cleaner. I am his friend, not his therapist." This is the attitude of women's liberation within marriage.

LEARNING EQUALITY

Susan came to our marriage with some androphobic tendencies, together with a big-sister complex and an orientation toward helping others. In analyzing our relationship, we learned what was necessary for us to establish a marriage between equals. Susan simply refuses to do anything she really doesn't want to do. At the same time, she's clear about what she wants and doggedly goes after it. She learned this approach because of her unhappiness when she blindly acquiesced to everything at the beginning of our relationship. Although her strong self-interest has given her some guilt, it has also been her strength. Not wanting to do housework, she found a way to afford help even when we were struggling students. She refused to relocate on behalf of Steve's career when this was expected of her. She insisted upon educational and travel experiences that seemed to be out of reach, but she made them happen. Although she is a good cook, she's maneuvered herself out of the kitchen. Susan gets what she wants for herself, and therefore brings no bitterness to our relationship. There is a lot of fun, happiness and friendship. She's generous, but it is her self-interest that has made ours a relationship between equals.

Steve originally expected to have a patriarchal marriage. Nearer in age to a sister, he is probably more comfortable with closeness than Susan. He has been a flexible friend, as we've grown from repeating the dynamics of our parents' marriages to creating our own way. It's not been easy—trial and error never is—but Steve feels he has personally come out a winner. Supporting his wife's development has yielded a second income, so he travels and is more financially secure than he ever expected to be. These are the benefits for feminist men who share the power *and* the drudgery. We share financial planning, parenting and yardwork. Housework is hired out as much as possible. Our household helper and a neighbor's catering business supply most meals. We've found that equality in a marriage is based on fairness about who does what, eliminating self-sacrifice by doing the unpleasant tasks together.

THE NEED TO BE ALONE

On a practical level, bonding without bondage requires time and space for your own pursuits. Single women are afraid of having their space usurped by eager boyfriends, complaining that although life is empty without a man, it's claustrophobic with one—the old complaint of "Can't live with 'em and can't live without 'em." The solution is to maintain enough separateness when you are intimately involved.

Partners should have friends and interests that don't involve the spouse. Each needs time alone. A man sometimes has trouble understanding this, and will feel that your retreats are rejections. Mindy wrote her fiancé the following letter:

Dear Scott,

As you know, I'm looking forward to our wedding next August, and I feel so lucky to have found a man who loves me as much as you do. Nothing makes me happier than being with you and planning our future. So I'm as confused as you are when there's an evening or an occasional week-end when I want very much to be alone. I want you to know that in needing time alone I'm not avoiding you, or feeling depressed, or have any misgivings about you. Being alone has to do with my own private relationship with myself. When I've taken time to be alone with myself, the thing I want most of all is to be with you.

Being alone is a kind of spiritual experience for me. It's a time of renewal when I sort out what's happening with me. You've asked me what I do, but puttering around in my apartment hardly describes what I'm really doing within myself. The urgent need to be alone that I feel isn't so that I can accomplish something external, but something internal. Because of the excitement of our plans, I need this time alone more than ever to catch up with myself and really appreciate what's happening to me.

When you let me have my alone time without guilt, you're giving me a precious gift. You're letting me be in touch with my own needs without distraction. You're letting me dream my own dreams. You're letting me become men-tally organized, serene and at peace. Your blessing on my alone time makes me feel especially close to you. In my opinion, it only comes between us when you object.

But if you can understand my special need to be alone, I know that you are my true friend and lover.

Love,
Mindy

How to Turn a Man into a Husband

When you accept a man for who he is, you'll become the person he trusts the most. You reach into his world and enjoy his pleasures, and from that place—that of an insider in his world—you can enlighten him about yours. When you fully accept the ways in which he's different from you, you can show him some of your differences. When he doesn't feel threatened, he will allow himself to be emotional and communicative. This is a gentle process, and is the way women help men, slowly, to regain some of the human feelings they have been denying.

The process is not the same as trying to change a man, because that intention is usually motivated by disapproval, not love. You can't get close to a man or have much influence on him unless you love him. In the fairy tale of "The Frog Prince," a maiden kisses a frog and he turns into a prince. When someone loves us, our potential for growth is released, and we become our best selves in response to love. When a man listens to a woman who cares about him, he is likely to want to please her and be attractive to her.

Some men seem to act more like frogs than princes. From the man who feels victorious after an argument in which he has demolished someone's ego, to the "chairman of the board" type, to the man who communicates with his family through grunts, sighs and silence (expecting them to read his mind)—it would be easy to catalogue the failures of insensitive, antisocial males. But that's not the whole picture. Men who act like frogs *can* be influenced. Most of them have no idea what they are doing, partly because their intimates maneuver worshipfully around their bad moods. Men *can* learn to be loving, and insight *can* replace blind spots. Kindness *can* flow where insensitivity once prevailed.

GETTING HIM TO HEAR WHAT YOU HAVE TO SAY

One of the best ways to work on a relationship is to develop sophisticated communication skills. There are many books on this subject, but to get you started, we will share some useful techniques from the field of Transactional Analysis. Some of the difficulties in communicating stem from the patriarchal marriage style that many of us observed in our parents. In these marriages, the man acted like a stern father, while the woman acted like a dependent child. Watch any movies from the forties and you will see a charming, innocent, breathless female with stars in her eyes and a strong, worldly male who "knows the score" and lets her know what the score is.

This Male Parent—Female Child dynamic can be reversed. There were clear areas of female expertise that reduced husbands of the past to bumbling children: sewing on buttons, baking cakes, polishing the silver and changing diapers.

Every person has a choice of three ego states from which to communicate: Parent, Adult or Child. Most of us grew up observing that Dad communicated as Parent and Mom as Child—except when they switched and Mom became the Parent to Dad's Child. What ever happened to the Adult ego state? Most likely Dad was an Adult at work, and Mom was sadly out of touch with her Adult function, since being a caretaker meant she was in her Parent ego state when she worked.

In creating a real relationship with a man, one in which you are communicating with him as an equal partner, we suggest that you both aim to be *in the same ego state at the same time* as much as possible. When he is acting like a Parent (a caretaker or a leader), you should communicate to him as another Parent.

Example I: Parent to Parent

JIM: I think we should take [daughter] Sara to Bermuda.

CAROL: Yes, she needs a good spring break. Maybe a theater week in London would be better for her course work this semester.

JIM: I agree that would be good for her.

If Carol had spoken from her Child ego state, she might have said: "But I don't want to go to Bermuda if Sara is coming!" Instead, she matched her Parent mode to Jim's Parent, which meant staying with leadership energy, and suggesting something she thought would work better for everyone. Jim was able to hear her as another Parent, not as a Child possibly competing with their own daughter for his attention. By matching Jim's authoritative role, Carol had the credibility that allowed Jim to fully hear her suggestion.

Example II: Child to Child

JIM: I just love the idea of a good golf game at that course in Bermuda, and then a swim in the ocean!

CAROL: Yes, and then we could have a champagne picnic on the beach . . .

JIM: Are you thinking what I'm thinking?

CAROL: Mm-hm.

If Carol had felt uptight about Jim's pleasurable fantasy, she might have replied as an angry Parent: "I don't think you should spend too much time on vacation playing golf. We should also have some picnics and some time alone!" Because she became a hedonistic Child while he too was being a Child, they could both listen to each other, and playfully communicate with one another. Carol not only matched his ego state, but captured Jim's playful mood, taking it several steps farther. It would have been damaging for Carol to act like a sullen child: "You only want to play golf and not be with me!" That would have made Jim feel he couldn't be a Child anymore, but was forced to be a Parent burdened with a wife he had to take care of. In the most satisfying intimate relationships, couples function a good part of the time as pals and playmates, not as mutual scolds.

Example III: Adult to Adult

JIM: It's going to cost a lot of money to go to Bermuda. I wonder if we can afford it.

CAROL: I was concerned about that too, and I made out a budget for the trip. With my expense account reimbursement, I think we're in good shape.

If Carol had responded in her Child mode, she might have pouted: "I need a vacation because I'm working too hard!" As Parent she might have chastised, "Stop being such an old tightwad and be more generous!" But she maintained Adult to Adult communication by keeping all of her comments informational and data-based.

When you match ego states you can be heard by the other person and there is no threat of a power play developing. Moving into the ego state of your partner won't keep you from saying what you have to say. When you consciously match his ego state, you choose to be effective. You are neutralizing the power dynamics so that your partner can respond to you best. When your communications are Adult to Adult you are colleagues, taking care of business together. When you're communicating Parent to Parent, you share leadership and the task of parenting. The emotional heart of your relationship is Child to Child, in which you are friends freely sharing hobbies, sports, travel and intimately exploring love, humor and sex.

Men and women have many differences, and skillful communication provides the necessary bridges across those differences. When you are on the same wavelength, it is a wonderful relief from the lonely space that too often divides people. All of us long to be close without giving up our differences, and that closeness can only take place when you enter the world of the other and get a feel for what it's like to be that person. Once inside, you must tell him about yourself in a language he will understand. Using the techniques of the ego states described in Transactional Analysis is a powerful way to describe your truth in a way that ensures his receptivity.

Going the Distance

To create a solid relationship it's very important to have an image of what you are building together. Essentially marriage means home. What you have together is a nest, a haven, a safe and welcoming place to be loved. Home is a spiritual place, although it exists in time and space.

Time must be set aside for the experience of "coming home," and a space must be created in which "homing" can happen. Today's woman resents housework, but she mustn't forget how much a relationship needs a beautiful environment to nourish the spirit.

The important factor in going the distance is having a goal, the mental picture of the lifestyle you want together. This picture must have an emotional component that nourishes you in a meaningful way. One of our own images is of sitting in our dining room with a white cloth, candles and flowers decorating the table. The kids have joined us, then retreated to homework, and we are there lingering over coffee—as we will still be doing in the years after they have left home. This is an image of a glowing ritual that we count on happening day after day. These moments are the *goal*. They are to be repeated, refined and anticipated.

Unfortunately, things happen to disturb domestic bliss, and married life is not all flowers and candlelight. Couples have trouble capturing those nurturing moments and experiencing their relationship as a haven. It's possible to achieve a deeply satisfactory, nurturing home, but you have to work through problems before it's fully achieved.

HANGING IN THERE

At some point in getting close you'll run up against a major impasse—that happens whenever people become intimate. You discover something about your partner you don't like. Or equally devastating, your partner focuses on something he doesn't like about *you*. One of you discovers an important need that's not being met by the other, or your partner has a habit or attitude that's absolutely maddening. What do you do?

If you want to create a real home, you must stay committed to each other. Threatening to leave will accomplish nothing. Working things out means that you approach your relationship as a system without an offender and a victim. It's a fifty-fifty operation. Even though it might suddenly seem as if one person is the culprit in the relationship, in marriage *two* people are always involved and there must be mutual responsibility for solving any problem.

The main obstacle is that the closer you get, the more problems you'll have to deal with. What many people don't realize, however, is that problems can be solved. You discover the art of intimate problem-solving by being both assertive and flexible. You may need to fight, express negative feelings and take an assertive stand about things that you refuse to tolerate. On the other hand, you must be flexible in terms of hearing the other person's point of view, lowering petty standards and dropping your own annoying habits. This is the process that goes on in successful marriages: two people learning how to live together in harmony.

It can't be achieved by grinning and bearing it. The answer is usually talk—hours and hours of dialogue until you figure out how to be happy together. This only works, of course, if there is a mutual goal of being happy. You must share the vision of the candles and flowers, so you know what you are fighting for.

LEARNING TO ASK

An intimate relationship is unlike anything else. A profound dependency develops the longer people are together. Patterns evolve and you expect your partner to meet your needs according to his particular talents, and he develops similar expectations about you. But because many things happen between you nonverbally, by way of habit or ritual, you can lose the skill of being precise and specific in communicating your feelings and desires. In many relationships the expectation develops that one's partner should magically give you what you need, intuiting those needs by reading your mind. That's often why a woman gets upset if her spouse doesn't give her the precise valentine or gift she wants, or do what she wants sexually. She must consider the fact that he probably doesn't even know what she expects. This insight may be no comfort to her, because she thinks that if she has to ask, everything is spoiled, but as an adult she must give up wishful thinking.

In intimate relationships, both men and women have problems being expressive, and specifically asking for what's wanted or needed. For a man, the noncommunicative stance is a way of being strong, since he feels vulnerable when he reveals a personal desire. He'll show he's angry if a need is not met, and will be even angrier if he must verbalize his need by asking for it to be fulfilled. When a couple works things out, they get their problem-solving systems in order. The primary one is learning to ask for what each wants, instead of accusing the other for not giving it. It's almost impossible to give to someone who is in a blaming mode, but it can be a real joy to give when asked or invited.

Going the distance means staying active on behalf of your union and your goals. Living in the context of a marriage can easily breed passivity, as if you regress to being a child who expects a parent to do things for you. Instead, you must be responsible, making sure that you achieve your goal of creating a nurturing home life together.

The Love You Give

The most mature form of love is generosity. In religion this is the kind of love God has for us. It's the love parents can have for their children, in which they enjoy seeing the development of another person. Witnessing the maturing process of someone you love and helping them to get their needs met can be very satisfying.

Generosity is the form of love that exists in stable marriages, and it is very rewarding to freely love each other in this way. Generous people live the richest of lives, because there is a self-renewing aspect to generous giving. In *The Art of Loving,* Erich Fromm describes this mature love as "wanting the best for others as well as for self."

Women who are primarily focused on intense self-development may not be aware that they are missing out on an important element of emotional expressiveness. They are filled with caution, making sure that they aren't being dominated in a relationship. However, they don't know how to initiate the dynamic of love and caring that will make equality the natural by-product of a loving relationship. Often they equate being generous and giving with being a "martyr" or a "doormat." Women today are counseled to be assertive and to define and protect their interests by clearly expressing their own points of view. They're primed to do battle on behalf of self-interest, believing that men never think in terms of equality. Their knee-jerk reaction is to be suspicious and to be defensive with men.

Many contemporary relationships have developed a lawyerly approach to working things out. Contracts are drawn up that make it clear who does what. The contract terms can be the source of continuing squabbles as couples argue endlessly about whether or not one is doing his fair share around the house. The problem with this good idea is it's so cold. It doesn't ignite the spirit of generosity between partners so that a natural spirit of giving grows out of deep concern for the well-being of the other. Instead, spouses rely on the *rules* of fairness to elicit generous behavior, and thus maintain a self-interested orientation.

The real question is how to join up and form a genuine love bond. Commitment means that you are signing on emotionally with another person. Your life is devoted to giving your spouse opportunities for happiness as well as making yourself happy. When you truly capture the spirit of generosity, it is easy and fun to give. You feel wonderful about your commitment.

THE RIDDLE OF THE GOLDEN RULE

Women are often marriage-shy because they mistrust their generous impulses. They assume that in the past women were *too* generous. Actually, what's frightening about marriage is not the generous giving of love, but rather the specter of turning into a docile child who hangs onto her man by pleasing him in every way imaginable. Generosity is *not* being childlike, blindly adaptable, or self-sacrificing: When you join a marriage partnership, it means that you each take one another's interests to heart. There is no conflict between self-interest and "other" interest, because of the deep respect for each other's needs. This is not an unrealistic goal, but one that really works. These are the mechanics of generosity that operate dynamically in a good marriage relationship.

What will happen when you are operating generously is that your partner's achievement of well-being is just as interesting and fulfilling as your own. That's why the uniting of another life with yours, embracing all of his struggles and successes, is so richly rewarding. The concept of selfishness or its extreme opposite, self-sacrifice, emerges only when the balance tips and a partner fails to focus upon both self and other. If one partner gets the balance out of kilter, the other person can be a corrective by refusing to shift balance.

Understanding and overcoming your fears will help you to release the loving, generous impulses that help you connect with a husband. Through the eyes of love, men will look different, the ones who are available will be attractive, their faults will seem less significant and you'll find points of contact. Your generous, loving instincts, once freed from past disappointments, can be very contagious. That's why women who have worked through their fears discover that they are free to get married. It's happened again and again with our patients.

The generous mode takes you out of your defensive approach to men. You lift the whole interaction between you to a higher plane. Amazingly, a generous woman is not vulnerable, because she is so full of herself. *Releasing your ability to love is ultimately the cure for androphobia.* As a giver, you direct matters and feel responsible for making things happen, instead of passively worrying about being a victim of disappointment. By taking responsibility you are completely released from the victim role. You learn that there is nothing wrong with loving a man like crazy once he's shown himself to be available and committed to you. Not being afraid to love is the key to no more lonely nights.

·14·
IT'S UP TO YOU TO GET MARRIED

Now that you know the role that unconscious fear has played in keeping you from getting married, how can you go about making the changes that will help you overcome your loneliness? The first step is understanding exactly what happened in your past to cause you to shy away from intimacy. The next is to consider what you can do today about the shadows those early experiences still cast upon your life.

Answering the Voice of Fear

As you make connections with your past and understand its influence, unconscious forces become conscious. Those inner mechanisms with their fear-based control over you are dismantled. You no longer have arbitrary, panicky, defensive reactions to closeness. Understanding unconscious fears is seventy-five percent of the job of overcoming their negative influence on you.

Once something unconscious becomes conscious, it loses much of its power to limit you. It's infinitely easier to contend with something feared in the light of day than in the darkness of night. You learn to say to yourself, "There I go again, thinking that a tall man will be scary like Dad." Or, "Just because he's in a suit and carrying a briefcase doesn't mean he'll ignore me like George did."

Hopefully, at this point in your reading, you can identify with the causes of fear that we've discussed and have made valuable personal associations to them. Now let's think about what else you can do to help yourself.

PERSONAL THERAPY

Through therapy we've seen many women overcome their mysterious avoidance of relationships that could lead to marriage. We've observed them letting go of fear, going through courtship and finally getting married. Like most people, you probably still have some work to do in becoming aware of your hidden fears after reading this book. If so, we highly recommend psychotherapy as a method of personal exploration. A therapist can help identify important aspects of your history that you are not aware of because of your need to hide your fear from yourself.

An important way therapy helps is through the process called mirroring. A session can be like looking in a mirror and seeing a clear picture of how you are feeling. Your reaction to this picture can take you in a new, positive direction. It's different from merely wallowing in your feelings when you are alone. A lonely woman in the supportive setting of therapy brings her loneliness into focus, senses it acutely and admits to herself, "I don't want to be lonely anymore." Emotional mirroring is a catalyst for changing your life, and it requires a helper. Soon after we help a woman in therapy admit to the fearful, negative part of herself that doesn't want to find a partner, she often flips over to the positive side and starts dating.

It was Freud who said that the purpose of therapy was to make the unconscious conscious. That's what we too believe is needed for you to overcome your hidden fear. It doesn't do much good to resolve that you're going to find a mate if you haven't worked on the emotional forces that hold you back.

FINDING SUPPORT

To overcome fear, you need as much personal support as you can get, and there are many ways besides therapy to find it. Classes, books, groups and friends are wonderful resources. Loneliness has a way of locking you into a disconnected, empty, helpless inner space. You must make distinctly conscious efforts to connect with all available resources to combat your fears of intimacy.

Withdrawal and introverted ways of spending your time aren't useful. Once you really begin to circulate socially, men will show their interest. A combination of working on self-awareness and staying in touch with good friends will help you come out of the shadows of fear.

Nurturing close relationships in which you share your feelings and listen to friends discuss theirs helps dispel some of your loneliness. If you are reaching out from a very isolated position, great neediness may surface and it's bound to frighten you. Be assured that in time increased contact with caring people will fill your emotional reservoir with many of the strokes you need.

By building friendships, you are building support for having a future partner. Good friendships keep you from burdening a potential marriage partner with excessive need for contact and reassurance, and they help you practice your skills of getting close to men.

IF YOU ARE STILL ANGRY

It's natural to answer the voice of fear with anger, but anger won't bring you the intimacy you need. With all of its positive impact, feminism often fans the flames of anger in male-female relationships. Today's woman is angry at men who haven't caught up with the strides that women have made. It's true that many men don't know how to relate to a self-confident, independent woman. But be sure that you aren't still wishing that a man be all-powerful, yet are ready to be very angry at him when he shows his strength! Women often put men in a terrible double bind: They're angry at them if they're weak and angry if they have any power at all. Getting over your anger means growing up, letting men be as imperfect as they are, learning how to be friends with them.

Your anger and fear will not go away automatically. You must work at not contaminating the present with your outdated anger, and you may need to dump it on someone from your past by expressing it to a friend, a therapist—or perhaps your diary. Yelling or punching pillows, and even bodywork such as bioenergetics or rolfing, can get some of the old poison out of your system. Ultimately, you must give up protecting yourself with your anger, because it doesn't protect you from your loneliness.

The key is to give up anger and cultivate love, which means consciously focusing on what you like in a man. In giving up anger, you tell the judgmental part of yourself to be quiet. Instead, you look for what is endearing, interesting and fine in your man. You should see him as a pal and as a fellow human being struggling along as you do. And when you get close, as a lovable teddy bear.

The Stages of Mating

In the past there were well-defined steps in our culture that led to the ultimate goal of marriage. These were formal rituals that supported a slow build-up of emotions, helping loving desire develop into a lifetime commitment.

Today the burden of mating falls upon you. It's your job to shape a relationship so that it will lead to marriage. That's the only way to stop being a victim of our times, when the culture no longer helps. Based on our work with men and women patients in the process of mating, we have developed step-by-step guidelines that we believe are essential to successful mating.

As you read through the following seven stages of mating, think of them as being like building a fire. You never start a fire by throwing on a whole log; you proceed slowly, adding small bits of kindling and waiting until each part catches. If this kind of early care is taken, a relationship can build into a roaring fire. As mating progresses, people's fears do inevitably come out. In the anxiety of uncertainty or androphobia, you might be tempted to throw yourself into the relationship too fast. This will smother the fire. Instead, step back and take your time. The slower you go, the more likely the fire will become well-established.

1. Observing Each Other from a Distance—In the beginning you play it safe, allowing your curiosity to be aroused and indulged with no revelation of your interest. You notice someone at work, at church or synagogue, in a class or on the bus and you take a good but discreet look. During this stage, you keep looking and you take your time—weeks, even months. You look to look, not to meet. While you look, you actually study a man, and learn as much as you can by observation, letting your intuition inform you about this person. Even if you talk to him, you stay detached and basically observe him.

The next part of this stage is also carried out at a distance. You do some detective work, finding out whatever you can about this person. You get help from a friend, if necessary. Sometimes it's a friend who first lets you know about a man you should keep your eye on. If so, gather as much information as you can about him.

During this stage, you can make yourself available

for being observed as well. The person you are watching might also be observing you—safely, discreetly, from a distance.

2. *Making Indirect Contact*—In stage two, you make indirect contact that does not reveal your personal interest in him. You may wonder whether this game-playing is a good idea, but these are all strategies designed to resolve fears. Courtship has always involved secrets; now the secret is simply your interest in him that awaits its best time of expression.

During stage two, focus all conversation on outside interests. You may connect around a work project, volunteer or charity work or a class assignment. This stage could take months. Essentially you are giving a man an opportunity for more nonthreatening observation.

Perhaps you feel impatient. You want to move forward impulsively or walk away. "Why doesn't he ask me out?" You agonize. But relationships need a gestation period. Through indirect communication you slowly build inner trust.

3. *Making Personal Meetings Formal*—The beginning of true courtship is when the relationship develops some personal contact beyond that which is based on a common outside interest. Personal interest has been developing below the surface, and now the desire to get together appears. This is a significant crossroads in a relationship: How you handle this stage can determine whether you are developing an affair or a marriage. The issue in stage three is: To mate or not to mate.

It becomes clear that the two of you want to enjoy each other's intimate company, not just plan the office charity drive. The task is to make your personal meeting into something formal. Usually the man wants to make it loose, like meeting you at a bar or dropping by your place. It's the woman who makes it formal. You don't just "get together"—you go to the movies, to dinner or a lecture. In the past our culture provided the norm of formality: dates, dances, events. Now it's up to you to shape things into dating by setting the requirements parents would expect in the old days—being picked up and taken home, and going somewhere specific.

The more formal things are, the safer you and your partner will feel. Formality creates a structure, a routine, something that can be repeated over and over again. Within a formal structure love and trust can develop. The next stages of mating are only possible when this structure has evolved. You need the right setting for the most important part of forming a relationship to take place.

Being formal requires effort, but it can catch on because it feels right. We suggest that you set the right tone by asking for dates, punctuality, planned functions, in contrast to sleeping in his apartment, spending the weekend together in bed or doing things impulsively. These are all fun, but they aren't conducive to marriage.

Of course, a woman can't superimpose Victorian mores on a man in the eighties, but gentle persuasion, friendly limits and candid descriptions of expectations will accomplish your purpose. Many men enjoy and respect challenges, and if you have expectations of a ritualized courtship, you'll be able to judge whether he, too, can get serious about structure. The man who picks up on this is someone who may soon be ready for marriage.

4. Talking and Communicating—In stage four, you move into the phase of really getting to know each other by sharing yourself, and listening to what he has to say. Communication, the heart of a relationship, has two parts: talking and listening. You must do both. Remember that the best part of you is your natural self that doesn't try to be impressive, but simply shares who you are, your history, your interests, your perceptions. This gives a man a chance to get to know you.

But it's your ability to listen that really gets things rolling with him, and will make him especially curious to then hear what you have to say. Some men are shy about talking about themselves, yet for others it's their favorite sport. In either case, the amount of time spent talking increases the depth of the communication.

As therapists, we can attest to the value of regular talk over a long period of time. If someone truly listens without judgment or giving advice, the speaker will go into great inner depths, often expressing with great relief what he really thinks and feels. This is the emotional mirroring effect—we can discover our true selves when we talk to another person. Everyone is grateful to a kind, attentive listener for making this process possible. Relationships are made of talk. During this stage you risk being self-revealing, and exercise your capacity to be a good listener.

It's important, however, not to cling or burden the other person with emotional responsibility for solving your own problems. Stage four is a time to discover what the other person has to offer, and to build positive mental images of each other that inspire trust and hope. Excessive neediness may elicit kind concern, but it will exhaust someone who hasn't yet connected to you in a romantic way, since the impulse to nurture is very different from the romantic and sexual energy necessary for mating.

5. *Adjusting to Each Other*—During this stage you ask the question, What am I going to do now about all the information I've gathered about this person? You may have discovered that the man you are seeing was badly burned by a divorce and has to develop trust in a relationship slowly. Are you willing to respect this and back off appropriately, keeping things formal in spite of the neediness you both feel? He has given you this crucial information, and you must adjust to it accordingly.

The period of adjustment is your response to the handwriting on the wall. You've got the picture. Suddenly you discover that there are differences between you, emotional or practical agendas that will require sensitive flexibility on your part. He's also spotting the problems and differences in you, but like everyone else, you'll probably discount *his* uncomfortable adjustments to you and be pained only by the prospect of your own.

This is a time when you both will be learning how to make changes. A woman who fears love must learn how not to let differences shut down relationships, unless those differences are serious character flaws. During this inevitable period of adjustment, the key is to stay positive. Don't sweat the small stuff. You may be afraid of making adjustments because you cling to yourself in your loneliness. But if you loosen up a little, the changes required by a relationship might turn out to be very good for you.

Simone learned how to back off when Phil was involved in a work project. Wanting this relationship made her curb her desperate clinginess, and she became much stronger emotionally for doing so.

Irene had to stop smoking in order to marry Pete, who was a health nut.

Pauline, whose job was nine to five, resented Alan's freelance schedule. But now that they are married and he is home taking care of their child, she is thrilled that she can stay with the job she enjoys.

Liz had to learn to be comfortable with Eric, a man who was more physically affectionate than the cold family she grew up with.

Sometimes the changes you must make are for your own good—but in the beginning you may not like what's good for you! You may be angry that you must bend for the survival of a relationship. Yet that's part of every married person's life. Inevitably, you will have to make changes and adjustments once you get to really know the person you are living with.

6. *Building an Us*—Talking and adjusting develop the groundwork for the next stage—building an Us. You develop an inner perception of the two of you as a couple, and a new approach to activities develops as you involve yourselves in Us thinking.

This is the phase during which you mentally pool your dreams, when you talk but don't do. You have fantasies of the future, which you gradually share with each other. You may rehearse marriage by shopping together, doing personal things for each other and thinking about what it would be like to get married, have kids, etc. You begin to think of the future on a time line, considering when you want particular things to happen.

It's at this point that many couples decide to live together. They try it out before they figure it out. We advise you to wait, because it's almost impossible to go backward. Living together can cause you to short-circuit the whole process and blow a fuse! There is still more patient work to be done in resolving inner resistances to marriage, and in intensifying desire through psychologically appropriate distance.

Marriage is essentially the building of a nest where you both will live. Get ready to build a good one. Prepare yourself carefully, so that you can really make it work. Paradoxically, the process of becoming an Us needs a clear sense of separation. You can only advance toward each other from a position of being apart. The human mating dance requires that you physically position yourselves far enough apart to correspond with the psychological separation that is yet to be bridged. Then you have space for moving together.

It's not easy to become an Us in these times. In our culture there is a strong focus on individualism and a preoccupation with the self. One of the results of the relationship revolution is that people are not interested in loving. Focusing on making it big financially, we are first and foremost encouraged to ask, "What's in it for me?" This approach can better your financial status, but it can limit you severely in mating. Self-absorption doesn't bridge the gap between people and establish the connecting bonds that are needed for mating. Self-thinking doesn't work; Us thinking does. You must drop your preoccupation with yourself and ap-

proach a relationship with the question, "What's in it
for Us?"

George fell in love with Amanda when she stayed
up most of the night helping him ready his sailboat,
which was going in the water the next day. Amanda
could have said to herself, "It's his boat. Why should
I make up for him being unprepared? I want to get
some rest so that I can enjoy the last day of my weekend."
Or she could have stayed up all night and then given
George a hard time the next day. We asked her how
she felt about helping him. "We were in it together,"
she said. "What's important to him is important to me.
We were both tired but happy the next day." They had
not yet verbalized their serious interest in one another,
but Amanda was operating out of the Us point of view
and thereby deepening their bonds.

A woman must have a concept of Us if she wants to
mate. When you are with a man, ask yourself, "Is there
an Us? Can we two people become a unit, a social
organism?" Asking this question screens out temporary
relationships, or ones in which you don't share values.
Then ask yourself, "Do I want to connect with this
person? And could he see me as his partner?" Convinced
that an Us is possible, you'll gradually share your dreams
of a mutual future. This can be a romantic period when
your unconscious mind realizes that your deep dreams
of love might come true.

7. *Ceremony*—This is the point at which all of the
formality and slow buildup of feeling reaches a commitment. It's definitely the big step. A marriage ceremony is a sacramental moment of sealing your
commitment to each other, a symbol that the Us has

been established forever. Formal marriage will support your relationship. You both want to count on it for the rest of your lives, and courtship has made you really want each other.

Before the ceremony of marriage, you have committed yourselves to each other in many little ways—by going out on specific dates, by sharing and by talking, by caring and listening. You committed yourself to the individuality of the other by allowing space between you. You have honored each other's boundaries through indirect communication, and backed off whenever necessary. Differences have been recognized and responded to by adjustment and flexibility. You have embraced one another's attachments. And a new entity has evolved—an Us, a couple committed to the bonds of trust, affection and need for each other.

Making It Happen

We can't go back in time and claim the old system of community and familial involvement in mating. We live in the singles era, and we alone are responsible for our own mating process.

The mating problem is a psychological one. If you have too many hidden fears, you will sabotage mating at the beginning or later on when the relationship gets close. Fear will make you pick someone who isn't available to become an Us with you. But if you want to mate, you'll go through a courtship process that is formal, and you'll be willing to make necessary personal adjustments. Your selection process will be focused in the right direction when you know that marriage is what you want, and you will be purposeful about getting it.

THE WOMAN'S TASK IN COURTING

In today's courtship you are faced with asserting your own expectations, and that means dealing with a man who will try to get things the easy way. When it comes to love, there is no easy way. Only acts of devotion and respect will create a loving psychological bond between partners. When you take charge of your courtship you do the very thing the culture used to do: You hold very high standards. A man who doesn't know how to court you must be helped and taught. There will probably be a significant moment of conflict when you deal with him in a way that surprises him. He must be aware of any significant mistreatment of you. A woman who is free of fear can be candid about this. Freedom from fear helps you raise your expectations and brings out the best in a man.

FREE FROM LONELINESS

In the story of Adam and Eve, Adam was lonely only for about a day, when his perfect partner was created. Biblical history assumes that we are coupled. Of all our human problems, loneliness for a partner is not one of them; God automatically took care of that by creating males and females. Many of us continue with this assumption, waiting for love to happen in the normal course of events. We somehow know that love exists, and we'd like it to knock us over with its power, to override and eradicate our fears, to prove itself to us, to comfort our lonely nights.

For these difficult modern times, it might help to look at another creation story, from the lore of the Navaho Indians: In the beginning, the Navaho people were about to leap from the underworld onto the earth's surface, but the men and women found themselves bitterly quarreling. So the two sexes separated. At first, the separations worked for each side, but soon deep problems occurred. Crops failed, and women's babies were born deformed. In the end, the two sexes decided they couldn't live without each other. They united, and when they did they emerged into a new, prosperous world.

We can't take love for granted. Men and women feel separated, and marriage no longer occurs in a normal, easy course of events. But it does happen when a woman breaks through her isolation and prepares to go through a mating process. It occurs when she maintains contact with a man she cares about in spite of her resistance to the process. By staying with a good prospective husband, in spite of resistance, you'll get to where you want to go.

There's always the temptation to throw in the towel just when things are getting good, when bliss lies around the corner from an argument you must have. Ambivalence always exists, running parallel to intimacy. In our society we live only in the present, expecting instant gratification, and we too easily forget how ambivalence is sorted out.

The lost art of getting married is really a maturing process of accepting the unacceptable, and of discovering that what bothered you so much wasn't so important. Because in marriage, something else becomes important: On a deep level, peace sets in and takes hold. It's the peace of an ongoing, lives-intertwined routine. It's who makes the coffee, how and when it gets made. Deep inside, you count on those moments of drinking coffee together more than anything in the world. This and crawling into bed together every night sustain you, free you from your loneliness. All the rest is the small stuff. No more lonely nights.

those boxes. These are just a few examples. I won't bring up certain other powers. They are so incredible, I'm not allowed to mention them.

This didn't happen by itself. Becoming a witch takes more than just having a gift. It takes a lot of effort. Like everything else, the secret is hard work. Young witches have a lot to learn. They have to read their textbooks over and over and practice under the tutelage of an older, experienced witch. Take me for example: I learned everything from my mother. She trained me, she corrected my mistakes, she made sure I was always headed in the right direction. It's thanks to her that I have become what I am: a true professional. When I do decide to give credit where it's due, I can admit I owe her a lot.

When it was my turn to be a mother, I was delighted at the idea of passing the gift of witchcraft on to my daughter. After all, what could be better than a child molded after your image?

I should explain that witchcraft is passed on from mother to daughter. Male witches may exist, but I doubt it, and I certainly don't know any. While I have met a few crusty old magicians who were retrained as jugglers, I have never met a man who was a true witch. Frankly, I don't think men and witchcraft go together at all.

What's more, witches can only pass their power on to their eldest daughter. That's why most of us are happy to have just one girl. And believe me, that's enough trouble for anyone. Honestly, if you aren't crazy about kids in the first place, what's the point of bringing up an entire brood of screaming brats with no future in the profession?

So one daughter is what I had. And the father, a guy by the name of Gerald—if I remember correctly—decided he wanted to call her Rose. *Rose?* What a name! Could he have thought of anything more boring?

I had no intention of giving him what he wanted, even if he was kind of cute. It wouldn't have mattered what name he gave her. I had put a spell on the birth registrar at town hall, and my daughter's birth certificate thus bore the name of Verbena, which you must admit is a lot more memorable and much more fitting for a future witch than Rose!

Now, I don't know if it was that episode or another that upset Verbena's father, but he sort of disappeared from the scene. Okay, I admit that I didn't make it easy for him. A few weeks after the birth, I moved out without leaving him our new address.

He looked for us for a long time. One day, we came across him wandering around our town, looking for us everywhere—in the town square, in the school, and in the library. As soon as I saw him coming, I surrounded us with a thick fog—making it completely impossible for him to see us. We could have bumped right into him on the sidewalk and he wouldn't have known. Poor old Gerald. Sometimes I think he's still looking for us.

For years I waited for Verbena's talents to reveal themselves to me. After all, it can take a long time for a witch's powers to develop. When witches are children, they are the same as all other little creatures: birds, squirrels, or butterflies. They laugh then suddenly become angry or determined or serious. They go from kindergarten to elementary school, attending birthday parties and dancing lessons. The little witches grow up not knowing what they are. Then suddenly one day—a day when they are in a terrible mood—they make their backpack fly across the bedroom, they walk past the florists and all the flowers die, they give jaundice to their school friends. It's witchcraft, but they don't recognize it, and these calamities take them by surprise. This is when the time is right—when they must start their education immediately. Wednesday afternoon dancing classes give way to witchcraft classes, and eventually, the little girl turns into a young witch.

That is what destiny had predetermined for my little Verbena. I watched as she grew up, always on the lookout for the slightest sign of something supernatural. But at eleven years old, Verbena was still depressingly normal. She was pretty and bright; she was popular, funny, mindful, and very kind. I was still waiting for the moment when she'd make the furniture fly around—but I realized that the only noticeable change was that she had started looking at boys.

"What do you see in that silly boy you're always talking about?" I asked one evening when we were drinking a cup of hot tea. She stared dreamily up at the ceiling and sighed.

"You mean Soufi? All the girls at school are in love with him."

"You, too, dear?" I asked, totally dumbstruck. "You're in love with him, too?" She smiled with her eyes half closed behind her long eyelashes.

"I don't know! All I know is that everyone says *he*'s in love with *me*."

There was no doubt about it, she actually cooed! That did it. My sole heir had turned into a lovesick bird-brain, which was all she had to show for herself at eleven years old. What a disappointment! I am not saying I was completely distraught, but definitely very disappointed.

2

$g$ood evening, Ursula," said my mother on the phone a few days later. "You don't seem like yourself. Is anything wrong?" That's Anastabotte. She has a knack for calling when I'm in the worst mood. You would almost think she did it on purpose.

"Right again, Mother," I replied. "There is something wrong. It's Verbena. She hasn't shown even the slightest sign she's a witch. I don't know if it's because she's dumb or just lazy . . . but she has discovered a *new* interest: the boys in her class! That's the *only* thing she's interested in. She's becoming so boring and normal—I'm beginning to wonder if she's really my daughter."

"No need to get so angry, darling," replied Anastabotte. Angry? You bet! Anastabotte was making me so mad, I felt like hanging up on her.

"Your daughter is going through a hard time, that's all. It isn't always easy being twelve years old...."

"She's *eleven*, not twelve!" I yelled into the phone.

"That makes no difference. Eleven, twelve, fourteen: it's always a difficult time. Kids are just trying to find out who they are! You should know that."

"Oh, come on! Nobody is asking Verbena to find out who she is! I already know who she is! She's a witch!"

"Don't be in such a hurry, my dear. Children don't always turn out exactly according to plan. Anyway, Verbena is still just a little girl...."

"*My daughter* is not just a little girl! She's never worn a dress, never had pigtails or ribbons in her hair. I've never given her a Barbie or any other doll for that matter. I have brought her up to become a good witch, one who is nice to her mother and knows her job, not one of those awful, bratty little snobs!"

"For heaven's sake," said my mother, "calm down Ursula. It's not such a tragedy."

"What do you mean, not a tragedy? My daughter is turning into a batty birdbrain, and you think that's not a tragedy?"

"That's enough," my mother cut in. "If the situation is so terrible, leave Verbena with me once a week. After all, I managed to teach you the basics, and Lord knows, it wasn't easy. Let me try my luck with her."

"Okay," I mumbled. "Come pick her up on Wednesday, the day she doesn't have school. And if you don't mind, stop bringing the *Lord* into it. It really gets on my nerves."

I put the phone down feeling both horrible and relieved at the same time. The idea of my mother and my daughter plotting together behind my back every Wednesday didn't exactly thrill me. On the other hand, knowing that I'd be rid of them both for a few hours each week was not unappealing.

After all, I suppose I'd rather have my daughter at my mother's than have her hanging around here and getting in my way. Verbena had picked up this habit of putting on a long face as soon as she woke up in the morning and keeping it glued on all day. Apparently, she finds my company profoundly boring.

"Come on, Verbena, what's the matter? Are you unhappy?"

"No, Mom, everything's fine."

"Are you bored?"

"No, I said. Relax."

She was lying so hard it made me feel sick.

"I'm not worried. I'm just asking that's all."

The long face gave way to a pitying glance, as if she was afraid of upsetting me. What insolence. My daughter now clearly considered me a sort of antique crackpot

whose heart might break if she wasn't handled with care.
When she thought I wasn't looking, she would glance my
way with a look halfway between wariness and disdain.
I was absolutely convinced that as soon as we found ourselves alone together, she'd get fed up with everything I
said and did.

"Why is it always just the two of us?"

"What's the problem, aren't we happy together?"

"Yes, but why haven't I got a father, someone I could
have dinner with?"

This is what she innocently asked me during one of
the long weekends that we spent hanging around the
apartment doing nothing.

"What a question!" I said. "That's the way it is. Our
families don't have men. And what would we do with a
father anyway?"

"Well, for one thing, he could invite us to go to a
movie and then out to eat."

"Well, if that's all it takes to make you happy, I'll take
you to a movie and out to eat. Get your coat and let's go."

"Okay," replied Verbena. She didn't say, "Great!" She
didn't jump for joy. She didn't thank me. She just got her
jacket and kept her long face. We went to see *Freddy,
Night Claws*. That was the first time the clever little minx
had ever asked me about her father. I felt a pang of

worry stab through my heart. First it was the boys in class, now a father. What had got into her?

For all these reasons I was quite pleased that Anastabotte would be taking her once a week. At least while she was with her grandmother, my daughter would stop dragging herself around in front of me like some sort of drama queen.

The whole class knows that Soufi is in love with me. When I think of poor Celine! She's crazy about him. Maybe I should tell her she's wasting her time. What do you think?"

For once, Verbena was in a great mood when she came home from school. She chatted nonstop at the kitchen table, and I listened with half an ear while brewing up a pungent potion for the dog next door. He wouldn't stop peeing on the door of our building, and I wanted to poison him. The nightmare! Just a spoonful of my pungent potion placed near the door, and I bet he wouldn't survive. After a few days of itchy skin and various other pains, the poor creature will give himself up to the devil, and the whole affair will be over! If the neighbors complain, I'll give them a dose, too. They're beginning to get on my nerves with their ghastly pets, anyway. I mean, do I let my black widow spiders pee on their front doors?

"Soufi is really weird," Verbena continued, gazing at the ceiling. "He's always looking at me and telling me I look like someone he knows, but he can't think who. Today at recess, he even asked the aide if I reminded him of someone."

Despite the concern I was hearing in her voice, Verbena seemed enchanted by the boy's interest. Poor kid, it was about time I set her straight.

"Can't you see this guy is just trying to make himself seem interesting? Saying you look like someone—it's the oldest trick in the book. Men have been doing it forever. It makes them look smart, and it's an excuse to start up a conversation. Don't fall for it, just ignore him; that's what he deserves."

"But I don't pay attention to him or to his dumb jokes," replied Verbena. "Really, I don't care what he says or what he does. He's really a jerk when I think about it." Suddenly she looked a lot less happy. She picked at her bowl of cereal with the edge of the spoon.

"By the way," I continued, "Grandma is picking you up on Wednesday morning."

"Okay," said Verbena, raising her face from her snack. "What for?"

"To have some time with you. From this week on, you

are spending Wednesdays at your grandma's. She'll be able to teach you something, and it will give me time to get some work done. Anyway, you're bound to have more fun with her than with me."

"All right," said Verbena. "But watch out—the soup is about to boil over."

"It isn't soup, you ignoramus!" I snapped. "For the hundredth time, it's a poisonous potion. Why don't you ever make the slightest effort to listen to me? You are exhausting, do you know that? Go do your homework. I've seen enough of you."

Wednesday morning, Verbena got up well before I did, and I heard her rummaging around in my bedroom. Her early morning bustling gave me such a headache, I had to bury myself under the quilt, nose to the mattress and pillow covering my head from ear to ear. But it did no good. I could still hear her singing the lyrics to a love song. . . . I glanced at the alarm clock. It was seven o'clock in the morning and Verbena's little tune was ringing in my ears like church bells. I really do hate the morning!

When Anastabotte rang the bell at eight thirty, Verbena jumped up to answer the door. I had to force myself out of bed, and once I had wrapped myself in my black robe, I joined them in the kitchen. To my astonishment, my mother seemed delighted at the prospect of taking my daughter for the day. As if nothing was quite so marvelous as the idea of hanging around all day with an annoying kid. Anastabotte had dressed for the occasion, and Verbena stared at her, speechless with admiration.

"Anastabotte," I asked, "where on earth did you find that outfit?"

From the depths of her wardrobe, my mother had dug out an outfit that clearly dated from her youth. She was wrapped up in a swathe of dark red velvet, a long flowing skirt whipping at her calves, and a sack-shaped top held her in at the waist with a snakeskin belt.

She had piled on makeup to match. Her eyes were half hidden beneath a layer of green eye shadow, and it looked as if blood were dripping from her lips. When she smiled, her yellow teeth lit up her white face with a strange amber glow. Her gray hair was stuffed into a net sprinkled with miniature black pearls. I bet she thought she looked like the picture-perfect witch, but I am telling you, she looked more like a crazy old lady.

All this didn't seem to bother Verbena in the least. She gazed up at her grandmother.

"She looks really pretty don't you think, Mom?"

"You think so?" I mumbled, collapsing into my chair in front of my coffee.

Horrified as I was by my mother's outfit, I knew I

could be happy about one thing: if Anastabotte had gone into her closet to dig out her old "uniform," it was because she meant business. No doubt she was going to see if Verbena had any potential … she might even be up for giving her a lesson. Then perhaps my little girl would stop being so fascinated by those snot-nosed boys in her class. She might give up asking me questions about her father, and hope against hope, she would finally become the perfect little witch I've always wanted.

Well, you can always dream …

They left at about nine o'clock. My mother swirled out in a cloud of red velvet and black pearls. My daughter was more soberly dressed in jeans with her hair combed so straight that it hung flat like a curtain. I closed the kitchen door and turned down the burner under my potion. Then I plunged into *Tasty Dishes with Crawling Insects*, an excellent recipe book that I can recommend to any housewife trying to cut corners.

4

That first Wednesday evening when she came back from Anastabotte's, Verbena seemed bothered by something. She sat at the kitchen table disheveled and red-faced, and I sat next to her waiting and hoping that she would tell me something about her day. I waited in vain; she told me nothing. For a long time, she gritted her teeth and stared into space as if deep in thought.

"So, Verbena," I began in a voice suffused with all the patience I could summon, "did you have a good day?"

"Yeah," she replied.

"Did Anastabotte spoil you?"

Another "yeah" broke the silence, then nothing. Not one word, until she burst out: "I wish I never had to grow up and become a witch!"

Oh no! If this was the result of her first lesson with Anastabotte, we would have to put a stop to it as soon as possible.

"Grandma says I have no choice."

There it finally was! Well it looked like my mother hadn't completely filled her head with nonsense.

"Anastabotte told me all about what you do, and I think it's pretty gross. I don't care about having magic powers. I just want to be normal, so why can't I?"

"Because you just can't. You were born a witch, and a witch you must become."

Verbena's head drooped, and her eyes filled with tears.

"Well, in that case, my life is over. I'll be forced to do all these awful things that are stupid and revolting. I'll always be different from the other girls, and I'll never be able to get married."

"And why shouldn't you get married, if that's what you want? You can get married as much as you like. You'll soon see that a husband isn't much use to a witch."

"But, Mom, that's just what I mean! I'll end up just like you. Oh, it's so totally unfair."

She shoved her chair back noisily, got up from the table, and stormed out of the kitchen slamming the door behind her.

Normally, this would have upset me. I would have got up, chased after her, and given her the slap she deserved. But what happened next was so incredible, I was glued to my chair.

When Verbena slammed the door with all her might,

she had no inkling of what was about to happen. The plates and dishes left their neat piles on the table and followed her out of the room! Quick as lightning, cups, glasses, and plates sped across the kitchen. This flying squadron of china and glass hurled itself in closed ranks against the door and smashed into a thousand pieces.

This brat had just broken at least two hundred dollars worth of dishes, and I'm not even thinking of the glass splinters I was going to have to pick up from the floor. I could have cried! But instead, I laughed. I chuckled with pleasure, rubbing my hands on my apron and gazing at the disaster with joy in my eyes.

Without realizing it, my daughter had just taken her very first step…in witchcraft! Only a first step, but a powerful one indeed! Her energy was so strong that she had started a revolution among the plates and cups! From that moment on, my daughter would be able to use her moods to transform the world! And if that isn't a sign of supernatural power, I'm a fairy godmother!

I called out sweetly to my darling daughter. "Verbena, honey, come here and look at this!"

"What is it now?"

Dragging herself from her room, she pushed the kitchen door open to the crunching sound of smashed dishes scraping the floor. Seeing the catastrophe, she raised her eyebrows and remarked acidly: "Are you crazy or what? Did you actually break it all?"

"No, my darling, you broke it! Congratulations!" I couldn't hold myself back. My maternal pride got the better of me—I swept my daughter into my arms and hugged her.

"Me? Are you nuts? I didn't touch anything! What is this, another one of your magic tricks?"

Verbena was shouting, I was laughing, and the downstairs neighbors were banging on the pipes with all their might. If they didn't like the noise, let the imbeciles move! For a moment I thought of cursing them and sending down a troupe of banging phantoms, but right now I had other things to do.

"Verbena, my sweet, don't you see? If those dishes followed you, it's because you have become a witch at last! You have power over things. From now on, objects will obey you—you only have to say the word!"

Verbena was outraged. She stamped her feet.

"But Mom, *objects* are fine just as they are. And they should just stay that way! I don't want to ask them to do anything."

"You don't have to ask them, darling. They understand by themselves. You were so furious, they must have felt it. Just now, maybe deep down, you wished you could have smashed everything in the kitchen."

"Yes..."

I could see her contemplating her innermost feelings.

"But I only thought about it; I definitely didn't ask for it!"

"Doesn't matter! The power flowed and everything broke."

"Oh, for goodness' sake!" said Verbena. "What can I do to stop it, I mean, this awful power I have over things?"

"Nothing, my treasure, I already told you. If you want to avoid problems, you have to learn how to use your powers, and to use them only when you actually need them."

Verbena stared into space as if she was thinking about something.

"You mean I can have anything I want?"

"Not so fast! If you ask for just anything, your power will turn against you. You have to know how to do things in moderation. Anastabotte can help you."

"Sheesh... sounds like a lot of fun," said Verbena, turning her back on me. "It's just another annoying problem. Great. Just my luck to have been born into a family of witches! It's not fair!"

She was on her way back to her room when she let out a deep sigh. The kitchen windows suddenly opened wide. A freezing draft came through the room, and the curtains danced in the wind.

"That's enough!" she screamed, turning furiously toward the windows.

The wind dropped, I closed the windows, and Verbena locked herself in her bedroom. The neighbors banged on the pipes again, and I tried to remember my spell for banging phantoms.

5

That night I struggled to get to sleep. I tossed and turned in bed, my tired mind went over and over images of all the years I spent raising Verbena. I may have a strong personality, and, yes, I am definitely brave, but it hasn't always been easy... to be alone every day. In spite of myself, I often envied ordinary mothers with their smug looks; mothers who walked through life helped out by their husbands. From time to time I, too, would have liked to have someone to lean on and to share everyday highs and lows. But fate had decided differently. Fortunately, my daughter's progress was going to reward me for all my trouble. My efforts had not been in vain.

In the morning, Verbena acted as if she had forgotten everything that had happened the previous evening. She carefully avoided talking to me, glancing at me warily now and again. Finally, she left for school with her backpack and relief in her eyes.

No sooner had she left than I picked up the phone to call my mother. I hoped that we'd be able to share the good news, since it doesn't happen often! But she didn't seem as pleased as I was about her student's progress.

"Anastabotte!" I cried proudly. "Verbena has finally become a witch!"

"Already?" she mumbled. "She's so young. I think we should wait a few months—or even a few years—before getting too involved with the real stuff."

"She isn't a fool," I answered. "She's a really bright kid, pretty advanced for her age."

"Be careful she doesn't get too advanced," my mother replied threateningly.

I shrugged my shoulders. My mother thought just because she had brought me up, she was the world's witch specialist. What a piece of work! So petty, so pessimistic and grumbling.

"Whatever your opinion of the whole thing, the bottom line is that now you're going to be in charge of your granddaughter," I said. "Next Wednesday, you can give her some exercises. It's time we began her training."

"Okay, okay," grumbled my mother. "We'll see what we can do. I'll ask her what she thinks. She's sure to have some ideas."

"Verbena? Ideas?"

"Your daughter is not as stupid as you seem to think," Anastabotte replied. "Why don't you try trusting her? And trust me, too. You'll see everything will work out."

"You could at least pretend to be pleased," I said, exasperated. "For once, I wake up in a good mood..."

At that point in the conversation, Anastabotte started invoking the Lord, nature, and other elements of fate. To put a stop to her ranting, I hung up on her. But looking back, it probably would have been better to have kept talking to her...

But even witches can't foresee everything. It took only a few days for my mother and my daughter to get in sync with each other and turn my whole life upside down. It makes me mad to think that in the end, they both made a fool of me. All I had ever wanted was my daughter's happiness and a little help from my mother.

PART 2
....

What Anastabotte Thought

(A grandmother's voice)

1

My daughter, Ursula, has many good qualities. For example, she is determined and hardworking. But she does have one big fault: she is cursed with what is commonly referred to as "bad character." Even as a little girl, she was hardheaded and stubborn as a mule, obstinate and unsociable. Don't tell me it's because she's a witch. Witches are like everybody else: some of them are joyful souls and some of them are sourpusses. My daughter is one of the sourpusses. I love her very much, but that's the way she is.

I have a pretty strong personality myself, but life has made me that way. I haven't had an easy time. I have lived through wars, suffered the loss of my husband, and worked very hard to bring up Ursula. I have had to fight my own battles and be strong enough to protect my daughter. But it's true that I have been rewarded by moments of real joy. One of which was the birth of my granddaughter, Verbena, whom I consider to be one of the great sources of happiness in my life.

And that name...*Verbena*! How typical of Ursula! She could have called her Lucy or Marie or Laura. But no, she had to be a smarty-pants. First of all, she ran out on the kid's father. He was a nice guy—George. Or was it Gilbert? Or it might have been Gerard, I can't remember. Anyway, he was charming and easy to get along with. Then, Ursula gave the poor child an impossible name. Luckily, Verbena is a marvelous little girl. She's even managed to make the name suit her...because believe me, it's no joke to live with a name like that. I know what I'm talking about. Even now, I regret that my mother didn't call me Julia or Simone, instead of weighing me down with an absurd name. Anastabotte, I mean, please! Imagine a young Romeo under the window serenading you. What could he use to rhyme with Anastabotte? Hot? A lot? Rot? No matter what, it's ridiculous, which is why no one has ever serenaded me under a window. I have missed out on that. But I'm not changing my name now; I'm far too old to be baptized again!

I have always adored little Verbena—such a sweet, kind, polite, pretty, and easygoing child. I'm not saying that her mother doesn't love her; Ursula does love her daughter very much. But the truth is, she has no patience.

She's got it into her head that Verbena will become a great witch. Even when the kid was a baby, Ursula would watch over the cradle waiting for the very slightest signs of witchcraft. Over the years, things got worse. She would look at her daughter quietly playing in a corner, then turn to me with consternation in her eyes: "Mom, don't you think that Verbena is just so ordinary?"

"How can you say that about your daughter? Look how lively she is! Look how well she plays!"

Ursula would shake her head, discouraged.

"Who cares that she knows how to *play*? Verbena has just *got* to become a great witch, and it doesn't look like she's headed that way!"

"She has *got* to, she has *got* to...she has *got* to do nothing at all, my girl. Verbena will do what she wants and by the way..."

At this point in the discussion, we would usually start screaming at each other like a couple of fishwives.

This went on for ten years as Ursula became more and more of a nervous wreck. All the while, Verbena was growing up. What happened when Verbena got older was unavoidable: she began to ask her mother questions. When she didn't like the answers, Verbena would get mad.

From then on, whenever I called Ursula on the phone, I had to listen to her complain about Verbena.

And I had to keep quiet. Whenever I so much as spoke, she would hang up on me.

One day when I'd had enough of this complaining, I finally let her have it. I told her, if it was so terrible, I would look after Verbena myself—once a week. To my astonishment, she accepted. You have to admit, when it comes to witchcraft, I've definitely got the goods. So that's how it came to be that on the following Wednesday morning, I rang their doorbell, ready to spend the day with my little granddaughter.

I had dressed up for the occasion. I had asked Madame Arsène—my neighbor and best friend—for advice. After lots of hesitation, we finally chose a velvet suit with a lizard-skin belt from my closet. I shook the mothballs out of it and put it on with feeling. It was the dress I had worn on my wedding day, when I married Gervais, Ursula's father. Looking at the dress, I was overcome with nostalgia.

"Well, well, Madame Anastabotte, you certainly did love your husband!" Madame Arsène said kindly.

So many memories... Tears filled my eyes, and I sat down for a moment to pull myself together. I'm getting too old to hide my feelings.

"Yes indeed, Madame Arsène, Gervais and I were made for each other."

"What a tragedy, dying so young and leaving you alone with your little girl!"

"But how lucky I was, Madame Arsène, to have known him and loved him," I replied.

With these words I calmed down. After all, what could be happier in life than marrying the one you love? And this dress reminded me of that.

I was worried the dress could be too small after all these years, but not at all; it slipped right on, as if I had worn it the night before. It was as if my dress was happy to be worn again. To do it justice, I put on a generous layer of makeup, rouged my lips, and left the house to fetch my granddaughter.

2

Verbena opened the front door. Her hair was neatly combed, and her clear complexion made me think of the springtime. Ursula, on the other hand, looked like the harsh winter. She had obviously just got out of bed: disheveled, wrapped up in her old bathrobe with dark circles under her eyes. She was really grouchy. I suppose she never has been a morning person.

While I poured her a cup of coffee, she looked me up and down. I watched an expression of horrified disbelief cross her face. She didn't like my dress; that much was clear. Ursula and I have never had the same taste in clothes. I might have told her the sentimental history behind my dress, but now was no time for a cozy chat. I gulped down my coffee, and we were off. I swooped out majestically with Verbena following hard on my heels.

As I closed the door behind me, Ursula mumbled a vague "have a nice day." I felt somewhat like a double agent, since I had no intention of inflicting witchcraft lessons on my poor Verbena. After all, the poor kid had never asked for anything! I simply intended to explain the basics of the job so that she would know what Ursula expected of her. We'd have plenty of time to do whatever she liked after that—either I would teach her what I knew, or we'd go for a walk and to a movie. All in all, I was just hoping we'd have a good time together.

I should tell you, I haven't always been this nice. When I was a young mother, I'd spend all night making Ursula study witchcraft. But I suppose as you get older you get less demanding. For my granddaughter, as for myself, I wanted nothing more than a simple life and a clear conscience.

We started to walk to my house. I live in a tiny two-story house on a quiet street. Inside, the kitchen opens onto a minuscule garden surrounded by walls where pear trees grow. At the beginning of winter, I prune them carefully, and in the spring, they're covered with a froth of white blossoms. By summer's end, the trees give enormous, firm, sweet pears, which I peel and have with my tea.

We had almost arrived when Verbena began looking nervous and then started slowing down.

"How weird," she said. "Those guys are from my class. How come they're here?"

In front of us were two kids in jeans and sneakers.

"Hello," the taller one said to me politely. "Hi, Verbena."

"Hi, Soufi," she replied, lowering her eyes. "Hi, Vincent."

"We're going to soccer practice," Soufi announced, although nobody had asked him.

Since Verbena didn't utter a sound, I replied for her.

"Well, we're going to my house. We're spending the day together."

"You're lucky your grandmother lives so close," said Soufi to Verbena. "I only see mine in the summer."

"Where are you from?" I asked, suddenly curious.

"From Brittany. My grandparents live in Plouermel. That's why I hardly ever see them."

And to think some people complain kids aren't polite! This Soufi was not only polite, he was genuine and nice. I found him charming.

"If you wish your grandmother was close by, young man, you can visit me. I live in the little house just between the stationers and the laundromat. All you have to do is ring the doorbell. Why don't you come this afternoon? We're having crepes, aren't we, Verbena?"

"Mmmm," she mumbled, burying her chin in her jacket.

"And bring your friend," I added.

"Thanks," the friend murmured, painfully shy.

"See you later," said Soufi cheerily by way of good-bye.

The two boys continued on their way, and I busily started looking for my keys. As I scrambled around in my bag to find them, I noticed that an unusual silence had fallen between me and Verbena. Since we'd run into those two boys, she had not said a word.

"What is it, Verbena, did I do something wrong?"

"Nah, it's just weird you invited them to your house like that. I don't know what to talk about with Soufi and Vincent."

"Don't worry, Soufi looks quite capable of keeping the conversation going by himself. Anyway, you'll probably be glad to be with someone your own age by the end of the day. You'll get sick of chatting with an old lady after a couple of hours."

"But Grandma," said Verbena, squeezing my hand in hers, "I couldn't be bored with you. Let me explain! At school, the boys don't hang out with the girls. We only hang out together when we play coed soccer. The girls in my class don't actually ask boys to come over! We just talk about them."

"What? And I thought the only thing you cared about was boys! I can see your mother was exaggerating *again*." This comment was just to reassure Verbena, you see. Deep down, I was rather pleased with myself. I had seen right away that Soufi was a terrific guy, and I also like meeting new friends.

3

"Now, my darling, your mother has asked me to explain a few things..."

We were sitting side by side on the green bench in my garden in the shade of the pear trees. Verbena shook her head, looking fed up.

"Yeah, I know she has her heart set on me being some great witch, even if I don't want to. What I don't get is why she can't just be a great witch herself—and leave me alone!"

"Oh, sweetheart, unfortunately you don't really have a choice. You were born a witch, and one of these days, you're going to realize you have powers. You'll just have to get used to it."

Verbena began to look more and more anxious.

"But don't you get it, Grandma? What makes me mad is, I can't even choose. It's no fair being forced to do things I don't want to do. I'm happy just how I am. I don't want to be like her. Why can't she just be herself if she thinks it's so great!"

"Don't make fun of your mother. You two have something in common whether you like it or not. She passed on her gift to you from birth. Even if she had abandoned you, even if she had never raised you, you'd still become a witch. That's the way it is. It's nature."

"Then I'll fight nature," retorted Verbena.

I put my hand on her knee.

"Then you've already lost. Nature always wins in the end."

"Well I'll fight it anyway."

She certainly was a chip off the old block. Looking at her furious expression, with eyes glaring at her shoes and fists curled up on her knees, I saw myself thirty years earlier with my rebellious, obstinate, pigheaded Ursula.

"Let's try looking at it another way," I suggested. "What is it about witchcraft that annoys you so much? Is it *only* because you don't want to be like your mother?"

This angle must have amused her, because she looked me in the eye and grinned.

"Well, actually, yeah. I sure don't want a pointed nose, cat's eyes, crazy outfits, and dumb powers. I just want to be how I am now."

"You know, you really can become your very own

kind of witch. Nobody is asking you to dress up, and nothing says you have to be an evil beast. You don't even have to use your powers. But you do have to learn the basics. And then you can do as you please."

Now Verbena looked relieved. She gave a sigh of relief, and I saw her shoulders relax.

"Are you positive, Grandma?"

"Absolutely, darling."

"Okay, then explain it all to me right now, and then we can go and have fun."

"Come on then, I'll show you my workshop."

We went down the narrow staircase that leads to the cellar where I have my workshop set up. I admit I hadn't been there for a while, and tall weeds were growing over the bottom of the iron door. The key groaned in the rusty lock, and the door opened slightly revealing a peaceful darkness. The workshop gave off a sweet perfume: a mixture of dust, dried roses, and mushrooms.

4

*I*n the last few years, I've gone down to my workshop less and less often. Now that I'm no longer working, I live on my pension. And if anyone were to ask me to show them some of my old tricks, they'd have to beg.

"Last time I came down here," I said aloud, "it was to do Madame Arsène a favor. Poor thing! She was quarreling with her husband so much that life was unbearable! She looked terrible, and her mood swings were awful."

"What'd you do?" asked Verbena, sounding slightly worried.

"Oh, plenty of things! Creams and lotions for her skin and hair, another potion for her digestion, and another one to stop her moodiness! Oh yes, and a one-year subscription to a funny magazine..."

"That doesn't sound like witchcraft to me," Verbena

protested. "Any old drugstore or magazine stand has that stuff!"

"Tsk, tsk, you silly girl. I am a thousand times more mysterious and a thousand times more efficient than all the pharmacists and magazine vendors in the world! First of all, I cast a few of the most marvelous spells on her house—so for a few weeks her life was a constant flow of pleasant surprises: Brazilian music in the morning, flocks of colorful exotic birds flying by her windows, a decorated guard at her front door, a fridge full of healthy, delicious treats, and so on. Believe me, things changed very quickly. Suddenly, she looked fifteen years younger, and she enrolled in an African dance class!

"Is *that* witchcraft? I thought it was only used to poison the neighbor's dog."

"Well that just shows how much you know about it! I *thought* you had the wrong idea."

"Not that wrong, Grandma! My mom spends her life making stuff just so she can drive the neighbors crazy!"

"You mean that's all she shows you. How do you know she doesn't do other stuff, hmm? Anyway, with all due respect, I don't think your mother's life seems to be going in a very good direction. I've noticed she hasn't seemed like herself for the last few months. Sometimes I think I should give her the same treatment I gave Madame Arsène."

We went down the stone steps into the cellar. In the semidarkness you could just make out tabletops with shelves in the walls above them. In the middle of the room, hanging above a small open fire, my distilling equipment reigned supreme.

"Could you turn on the light? The switch is by the phone, on the right near the door."

The lightbulb crackled slightly, but it worked. I looked around and felt satisfied. Apart from a threadbare rug layered with dust, the workshop was in good shape. I'm never the type to leave a mess—and I always take good care of my workspace.

"Look how clean everything is," I said to Verbena. "I always used to tell your mother that her workshop should be as spick-and-span as a secretary's desk."

"Ugh!" was Verbena's reply.

I noticed she was looking around my workshop with her eyes popping out of her head.

"What on earth is *that*?" she finally asked, pointing an accusing finger toward the wall.

"Oh, those are my little bats. You split them in two and leave them to dry. You know, dear, to preserve them. Don't they look cute, split right down the middle? They almost look like miniature coats, specially tailored for gnomes."

"What about those things in the jars up there on the shelf?"

"Hmmm, those are mandrakes in formaldehyde."

"Ugh, it's gross. They look like little monster men with roots."

I cleared my throat, feeling a bit awkward.

"Well, in a way, that's what mandrakes are. They are half vegetable, half something else. You know, they make a noise when we dig them up. Funny, huh?" I added in a whisper.

"Foul," said Verbena. "Don't tell me any more. I already feel like puking."

I didn't want to say anything else about mandrakes. It's a difficult subject. Mandrakes grow wild at the foot of gallows and trees where the corpses of hanged men have swung. I must admit, if you're not used to it, it sounds quite revolting. But it's nothing to get worked up about. Nowadays you can buy mandrakes straight from Dutch hothouses . . . they even sell synthetic ones.

However, my granddaughter was not in the mood to listen to my lecture, so the less I said, the better. In fact, I began to feel less and less certain that showing her the workshop had been such a good idea.

Verbena inspected everything, from my jars of insects to my jars of snakes. Now and again her eyes would rest on posters showing sketches of deformed bodies. Her gaze traveled across bear claws and rows of birds feet suspended from the ceiling in order of size. Luckily,

I had given up breeding these creatures! I could just imagine her expression if she saw cages crawling with scorpions, rats, or poisonous centipedes....

Among the tins of powder (plants, bones, minerals, organs) I noticed a tin of tea. I picked it up and grabbed a jar to boil up some water.

"How about a nice cup of tea, darling?" I suggested. "Darjeeling?"

"Not on your life!" Verbena yelled.

She sat down heavily on a stool, as if her legs had suddenly become too weak to carry her. Poor dear, her nerves were in shreds.

"But, Grandma, how can you work in such a disgusting place? You're such a sweet, kind lady!"

I adore it when my granddaughter tells me I am a "sweet, kind lady." When I die and go to heaven, to meet God sitting with all the good people, they'll weigh my soul to see how heavily I've sinned, and I will remind them that for Verbena I had always been a "sweet, kind lady." I'm sure they will take that into account. I don't expect to get a mansion in heaven, but I can definitely see myself with a small apartment up there, somewhere near the entrance to the Garden of Eden, where there's a nice breeze.

"Oh, you big baby!" I said cheerfully. "I don't see what shocks you so much about this place."

"What! Just look around! People seeing this would think you had purposely collected all the most repulsive and freakiest things in the entire world. What could you possibly do with it all?"

"Believe me, I can do a lot of amazing things."

"But what can you do that's good—that makes people happy, I mean?"

Poor kid! She certainly had plenty to learn! It would be up to me to show her that things are not as simple as they seem. Out of the shadow, we can sometimes make light.

"Sit still on that stool for five minutes, and I'll show you what a good witch can do with all these horrible shriveled things in jars, then you can judge."

I wanted to do something attractive, simple yet spectacular. I decided on the blue shadow trick.

5

To be quite honest, I am no longer very good at remembering all my old recipes. As you get older, your mind gets rusty, and I was definitely out of practice. I'd have to dip into some of my old books to refresh my memory.

From my earliest days as a witch, I always wrote everything down in sturdy, hardcover notebooks. These notebooks now contain the whole of my knowledge. Truly, they are a rare treasure of information. Ursula has often asked me to give them to her, and I have always refused.

What you won't do for a daughter, you are willing to do for your granddaughter. Verbena's birth changed me, melting my selfishness away. I decided I would leave my notebooks to her, and had written in my will: "To Verbena, I leave the five large notebooks entitled *Anastabotte's*

Tricks and Tactics. I know she will take great care of them, in honor of my memory."

The parchmentlike paper was crisp in my fingers. It exuded a welcome odor of nocturnal conspiracy. What a pleasure it was to make these ancient gestures again. In the second notebook, I found my spell. Just as I remembered, the blue shadow recipe called for a number of revolting ingredients, for example: mandrakes, poisonous centipedes, various types of drool, and other bodily fluids (I will spare you the details).

Full of nostalgia and excitement, I found myself humming as I reached up to the shelves for all the necessary ingredients—animal, vegetable, and mineral. I took some hair, some horn, and some sap. I cut, grated, and crushed. I cooked, boiled, and fried. I mixed, separated, and distilled. Indeed, my instinct for just this type of witchy "cooking" returned, and by the time it was finished, I was a red-faced mess, with my hands completely coated in brownish goo. I must have looked possessed.

"I'm nearly done, dear."

She was sitting motionless on a stool, watching me with a mixture of wonder and suspicion.

"You're nearly done with *what?*"

Poor girl! I had gotten so carried away with everything, I had forgotten to tell her about the blue shadow.

"I'm going to make this sort of remote-controlled

dream, and we're going to send it to someone. When it reaches this person, a blue shadow will make him or her disappear for a few seconds in a colorful whirlwind. It feels nice, looks pretty, and it's completely harmless! Who do you want me to send it to?"

"Um...I don't know."

"Hurry up! It's ready!"

"Okay, send it to Soufi."

A thick cloud of beautiful lavender blue smoke began to rise up in the distilling jar. Flowing gracefully like a living being, it curled through the long glass neck, where I was waiting for it. Waving my arms like a conductor, I guided it on its way, chanting a spell containing Soufi's name.

Instead of fading away into the room like a regular smoke ring, the blue shadow stayed in one piece, glittering with a thousand shades. It danced in front of us for a moment before leaving the workshop, floating through the walls as if they were not there. Then I rubbed my hands on my apron, pushed my hair back out of my eyes, and asked Verbena nonchalantly:

"Well?"

"I've never seen anything so magical in my life," she admitted.

"Now do you understand...with all these things you find repulsive and morbid, we can work wonders?"

"I don't know," she replied. "I'm a doubting Thomas—I only believe what I see. I have to wait till I've seen Soufi."

"Just remember, my doubting Thomas, the power to make dreams come true is within your reach. But if you want it, you will have to take it."

"You just won't give up, will you?"

It was clear that my little Miss Suspicious wasn't going to be convinced by the first trick she saw. I cleaned the distiller, put away my jars and tools, and took off my apron. Then I walked proudly toward the door.

"Come on, my girl, let's go upstairs. I've done enough amazing demonstrations for today. Now it's time to make lunch.

We returned to the daylight, fixing lunch, talking of this and that. We ate sitting across the table from one another, and afterward, I suggested that Verbena go play in the attic. She spent hours searching through the closets, looking for old photos, clothes, and all those curious things that accumulate in no particular order during a lifetime.

As for me, I sat in the living room in my favorite leather armchair, with an open book on my lap.

I was just dozing peacefully when the doorbell rang. I jumped and looked at the clock. Four thirty, teatime—it must be that boy in the street I'd invited that very morning. Soufi was his name. I had almost forgotten all about him.

6

When the bell rang, I heard the thumping of feet on the stairs, then an abrupt stop. Verbena had probably rushed down to open the door and decided halfway down to let me do it.

"I'm so glad you came," I said to the young boy standing on the doorstep with a winning smile. "Isn't your friend with you?"

"Vincent is very shy," Soufi replied. "And his mom doesn't like it when he's invited to eat with people she doesn't know. You okay, Verbena?"

My granddaughter had finally decided to finish coming down the stairs, and she was walking down the hall looking aloof.

I took the kids into the kitchen, sat them down at the table, and got a bowl of crepe batter from the fridge. Sitting next to Soufi, Verbena contemplated her nails with enormous interest. Actually, we were both waiting for Soufi to bring up what happened to him that afternoon, when a sort of blue tornado . . .

"So, did you have a good time at practice?" Verbena finally asked nonchalantly.

"Yeah," Soufi replied. "The coach is great but . . ."

The boy clearly had something on his mind. He frowned and seemed as if he wasn't sure he should say what was bothering him. Finally he let it out.

"You know, something totally awesome happened to me."

"It did?" croaked Verbena, while I watched the butter turn black in the pan.

"Tell us about it," I said encouragingly, taking the pan off the stove before it caught fire!

"But you'll think I'm crazy."

"Join the club," Verbena said. "We're used to weirdoes here, I mean we . . ."

"Well," continued Soufi, "I was sitting on the bench watching the game, when I saw a kind of column of blue smoke coming toward me, like a tornado. It headed straight for me, like it was looking for me, like it knew what it was doing. I wanted to run away, but I couldn't move. Once it got to me, it wrapped itself around me. Inside, it was warm and cozy, with a nice smell and rainbow colors. I was floating inside it like in a dream. Then suddenly, it all stopped and I saw I was on the ground, sitting at the other end of the field, staring right up into Kevin's face—he's my friend—he looked amazed!"

"'What's this, some kind of prank?' Kevin asked me. 'One minute you're over there, the next you're over here—are you faster than the speed of light, or what?' The others were too busy with the game to notice, but Kevin couldn't believe his eyes. He was shaking his head like I'd just played a trick on him."

"'Oh, you think you're a magician now, or something?' And he kicked me in the back. 'Go back to the bench, Houdini.' The whole thing had only lasted a couple of minutes, but it felt like I'd been kidnapped by martians."

The whole time Soufi was talking, neither Verbena nor I spoke one word. Verbena smiled cheekily, looking straight at her friend. I kept on gaily tossing crepes, which flew across the kitchen like thin stingrays.

Soufi stopped talking and looked at us astonished. I suppose the two of us must have looked odd, staring at him with silent fish eyes.

"Unbelievable!" said Verbena to break the silence.

"Maybe you walk in your sleep," I suggested. "You fell asleep, and while you were dreaming, you took off to the other end of the field."

"Could be," said Soufi. "Could be . . ."

I put a successful crepe down in front of him. It was crispy on the outside and soft on the inside.

"Sugar?"

The three of us stuffed ourselves until we couldn't eat another bite. Then I suggested that Verbena show Soufi the attic.

"You mean the attic, Grandma, right? Not the cellar!" she called, giving me a wink.

The two children disappeared upstairs, and I tidied the kitchen until it was time to take Verbena home. At five thirty, Soufi knocked on the kitchen door.

"I've come to say good-bye," he said holding out his hand and staring just under my nose.

"Good-bye, dear," I replied shaking his hand. "Good-bye," I said again, waiting for him to leave. But the big booby didn't budge. He stayed there, stuck, looking at me as if I was the eighth wonder of the world. Then he turned toward Verbena and looked intensely at her.

"Verbena doesn't look much like you," he finally said. He seemed disappointed. "Maybe she looks like her mother."

"No, she doesn't," I said. "Not really."

"Her dad then?"

"Please don't bring that up."

"Sorry," said Soufi, with an embarrassed smile. It's

just that I get the feeling Verbena looks like someone I know. I can't put my finger on it."

"Never mind, my dear, we all have our little fixations. But hurry home now or your mother will be worried.

That evening on her way back home, Verbena slipped her hand into mine.

"You know, Grandma, I really had fun today."

"I'm delighted to hear it, darling."

"But I still don't want to be a witch. I don't want to have any kind of lessons. I'd rather it was you who did the tricks. Would you mind?"

"Sure, it's up to you. So long as you're happy..."

"I am," she said, tripping lightly along beside me. "I'm really happy. I've never seen anything as cool as that blue shadow. Can we do it again next Wednesday?"

"We'll see," I answered.

When I left her with her mother, I was more than a little pleased with myself.

7

The following morning, I was glancing through the newspaper, drinking a nice strong coffee, when the telephone rang. To my surprise, it was Ursula. I looked at the kitchen clock. It was eight in the morning, which was early, much too early for her. On the other end of the line, her voice was trembling with excitement.

"Anastabotte, you'll never guess . . ."

The previous evening, Verbena had managed to break all the china—all because of a simple mood swing. As if that weren't enough, she had summoned up a fierce wind, which raged against the apartment windows. This proved, according to her mother, that Verbena had just shown the first signs of witchcraft. In my opinion, it was a bit too soon. For a kid who had absolutely no ambition in that direction, this was all a bit premature.

"The important things in life must not happen too

early," I remarked. "Everything in good time, neither too early nor too late . . . thanks to God, nature, and . . ."

"For goodness sake! Will you stop mentioning God every five minutes?" Ursula screamed.

She then hung up on me—again.

The following Wednesday when I came to fetch Verbena, she gave me a lukewarm reception. She vaguely said hello and blew me a kiss with a fake smile stuck on her face. I could tell—my granddaughter didn't trust me. She obviously thought I had been involved in the dish-breaking incident and that I had a hand in these powers, which had come to her out of nowhere. But I didn't have the slightest intention of talking about it in front of Ursula. I waited until we were outside.

"I assure you I had nothing to do with it. It just happened that's all. It's nothing to get upset about."

"And why can't I get upset?"

"Because it's not worth it. What are you so angry about anyway?"

Verbena threw me an accusing look. Her voice broke slightly. I had the feeling she was close to tears.

"I just wanted to be normal, meet a boy, fall in love, get engaged, and get married. Now all of that's impossible. I'll become unbearable, always brewing up spells behind people's backs! And nobody will like me. I'll be alone for my whole life, just like Mom."

The poor girl seriously thought that her mother was the archetype for all the witches in the world. I adore Ursula, of course, but even I can admit that for a kid of eleven, she would make a rather depressing role model.

"Silly girl," I said. "Nobody can make you live alone. You are free to behave exactly as you like. You are pretty and kind, and even if you are not always brilliant, I promise you, you will meet a nice boy who will make you very happy."

"What do you mean I'm not brilliant!" Verbena wiped her eyes and laughed.

"Take me for example," I said. "I got along beautifully with your grandfather. Unfortunately, he died too soon for you to ever know him—when your mother was still a little girl. If you want to know about him, ask Madame Arsène what she thought of Gervais."

"But I don't have a dad. Why don't I?"

"Because your mother is stubborn as a mule. I think she did love your father, but one fine day, God knows why, she decided to get rid of him. She would never admit it, but I'm sure she regrets it."

"It's her fault," said Verbena. "I'll never be like her."

"You'll be however you decide to be, and if the way Soufi looks at you is anything to go by, I bet you'll soon have more boyfriends than you know what to do with."

"Yeah, right...." Verbena snorted, lowering her eyes

modestly. "Soufi has nothing to do with this witchcraft stuff."

Two hours later, we were both in the flower garden bent over pulling weeds. I listened to the neighbor's doves cooing, I felt the lovely spring sunshine on the back of my neck, and I was thinking what I'd make for lunch, when Verbena announced: "I asked Soufi to come over for a snack. Is that okay?"

"Of course. But first I was hoping we could have a serious discussion about what you're going to do with your powers. If you like, I could teach you some spells. To start, I'd be happy teach you the blue shadow, unless you've got a better idea."

"That's just it. I do have an idea. I wanted to ask you..."

"Don't ask if we can time travel or that sort of thing. We're witches, not characters in science fiction novels, okay?"

"Yeah, I know that. But I'm not asking for anything crazy. I just want to find my dad."

"What?"

"Well, that's what I want. It can't be so complicated. All we have to do is make a kind of blue shadow that can search around for specific things, and..."

"Not so fast, my butterfly! If your father is still alive, we will find him sooner or later. But imagine how your mother will feel if she sees you strolling around with him? Have you thought about how she'd react? And what about him? Do you think he's really going to be so delighted to find us after all these years?"

Verbena shook her head stubbornly. "Why should I care what they think? My dad is my dad, and I have the right to know who he is."

She uprooted the dandelions that were invading my impatiens. Some kid, she could pull out weeds like a champion gardener. And as for her latest request, it made sense. Now that she was a witch in her own right, nothing could stop her from setting off in search of her father. And I certainly didn't feel like I had any right to stop her.

PART 3
·················

What Verbena Thought

(A daughter's voice)

1

She could at least have called me something cute, like Violet or Daisy, but no, she had to go and pick Verbena. Sometimes I think about filing a lawsuit, but other times I love her, and I wish I could take her on a fantastic vacation to Honolulu.

Nothing is more exhausting than a mom, especially since I don't know a thing about dads.

I've always lived with my mom. Before it was fine—no complaints, just the opposite, really! True, she was a little weird—she wasn't like my friends' mothers. In a way that was a good thing. She was sort of strangely alluring, she had a truck driver's mouth, and she'd take me to the movies anytime I wanted. But the fact that she was a witch also had a downside. She spent forever in the kitchen mumbling over the pressure cooker while she watched these repulsive brown mixtures bubble away.

The apartment was stinky for days, and one catastrophe after another struck our building. Water leaked on every floor, neighbors' dogs were suddenly struck down dead, and entire families broke out in rashes. So most people in the building would just give us angry looks.

Just to make things better, I started keeping her away from school. If I had let her do what she wanted, she would have gotten way too involved in everything at my school—especially since she didn't like the principal or of any of my teachers. As long as she stayed away, I could pass for a normal kid.

All in all, we got along well. There were times when we even had fun. When I was little, she did loads of great things for me: making birds come and eat out of my hand, changing the color of my dresses with the twinkle of an eye.... She made sure there were always plenty of other kids around when I went to play in the park. I always won games of hide-and-seek. Halfway through the afternoon, she would give out mint-flavored ice-cream bars and skull-shaped candies. We were so happy together that I never needed anyone else. She was enough.

Things started going sour when I got older. She decided to make a witch out of me, and from morning to night, she would give me these creepy looks and would talk about all the hopes she had for me. She was completely obsessed. A few weeks of this and I realized

I'd lost the mom I loved, the one who was so fun and patient. She was replaced by a new mom who was tough on me and super demanding.

I stopped telling her about my day at school, which had always made her laugh. She no longer listened to me, no longer saw me, and no longer understood me. When I talked about my friends, she rolled her eyes. I remember one night she was being really mean about Soufi. At this point, we didn't know one another so well yet. I was just really excited that he had noticed me. But in less than two minutes, mom managed to tell me that he was a phony, stupid dope who was taking me for a ride. At the time, I just wanted to cry. That's when I learned to keep quiet.

But I started to get more and more bored. The park is for little kids, and you can't spend your whole life at the movies. I was stuck inside the apartment with her, hanging out doing nothing every afternoon. I'd never invite friends over. First of all, she probably wouldn't have liked them, and anyway, I didn't want them to see her cooking stuff up in the kitchen, yammering to herself over the pressure cooker, dressed ridiculously with a scarf wrapped around her head, surrounded by weird-looking vials and dead insects (when it wasn't something worse).

I wanted to be like normal families—father, mother, and two or three children who only have to be helpful at home and good at school. To start with, I didn't have a dad. Why? A total mystery. My mother didn't think it would be a good idea for me to have a dad and didn't see the point in explaining. After spending the weekend hanging out in the empty apartment, I'd be completely depressed by Monday morning. It took me a whole day of school just to start to feel okay. Thank goodness there's school—to help us get away from our families.

Basically, I think I have a good personality, but to protect myself, I have become distant, sarcastic, and sometimes nasty. Luckily, I have my grandma. She lives near us, and her house is where I hide. My mom and my grandma fight a lot. That doesn't mean they don't care about each other, but they just can't help winding each other up. Lately, I've been the main reason they fight. My grandmother defends me, and that annoys my mom. So now almost every time they speak, the conversation ends in some stupid drama!

⊚ **2** ⊚

A few weeks ago, mom and grandma got together and plotted something behind my back. Grandma was so sick of hearing my mom complain about me that she offered to take me once a week, on Wednesdays, the day my school is closed. At first I was glad, but soon I realized the real reason behind these days with Grandma—to turn me into a witch just like them. Grandma pretended to be on my side, but a leopard doesn't change its spots. The whole time she was being nice to me, all she was thinking about was getting me to be exactly like mom.

Why worry about these conspiring relatives? I can take care of myself. Anyway, it turned out that the first Wednesday was really pretty fun. Even when she's teaching me witchcraft, Grandma always manages to surprise me. In the morning, she took me down to her workshop for the first time. If she wanted to shock me, she sure did it.

That workshop! If you haven't seen it with your own eyes, you can't possibly imagine how vile it is. In a corner of her cellar, my crazy grandma had collected a bunch of garbage even the trash collectors would refuse. Her collection of horrors ranged from the dried corpses of insects to the stinking syrups that my mother always uses in her concoctions. Anyone seeing the place would think they'd walked into the haunted house at the fair.

When she showed me around, Grandma had this proud look on her face, like a little kid. I didn't say anything. I just sat on a sticky old bar stool and let her go flitting around from corner to corner until she got tired of showing me everything, and we could go back up to the garden.

That's when she surprised me. When she saw that the workshop hadn't convinced me to become a witch, she did a demonstration. She leafed through her old books looking for a magic trick that wouldn't be dangerous— and she came up with *the blue shadow*.

Even though I wouldn't touch witchcraft with a ten-foot pole, I would give anything to get a closer look at Grandma's books. First of all, because they are beautiful. They are handwritten in ink on thick parchment pages and have lots of illustrations. Some are color drawings, and others are drawn in black ink. Second, I adore recipe books. Reading them gives me the best feeling—like I can make or do anything I want. I feel this way about recipe books, embroidery patterns, and gardening books. But I doubt I will ever have time to take a good thorough look through Grandma's books. I know my mom has already asked for them. Grandma won't let them out of her sight, even on loan. I don't stand a chance.

But back to the blue shadow. Grandma got it into her head to make this sort of blue ghost appear from one of her distilling gadgets. According to her, this blue ghost could be guided toward somebody and make them disappear for a few seconds. So it is one of those tricks that takes ages, is incredibly complicated, and serves absolutely no purpose.

Outside, it was warm and sunny, and I was really pretty annoyed at having to stay in the cellar all day watching Grandma stir up her foul mixtures, especially since she wasn't even wearing gloves! But I have to admit, it was worth it. When the blue shadow was done cooking, it rose up out of the jar and started dancing around the cellar. Then it finally floated out straight through the walls. I was speechless, literally glued to my stool. It was so pretty! I would have loved to disappear for a few minutes wrapped up in the folds of that beautiful blue cloud.

But just then, Grandma got into a panic. She was so proud her trick had actually worked, she had forgotten to choose who to send it to. She told me to pick a victim. I wasn't the least bit prepared, and thought fast. The name *Soufi* escaped from my lips with a vengeful smile. And that is how Soufi came to be the victim of witchcraft one Wednesday morning in the middle of soccer practice. Luckily, he was only sitting on the sidelines at the time.

I thought of Soufi because we had run into him and Vincent in the street that morning. I was pretty embarrassed to see him outside of school, especially since I was holding hands with my grandma in her red velvet outfit. My slight embarrassment turned into total confusion when grandma decided to start a conversation with them. Soufi, who isn't exactly shy, told her his life story, right there on the sidewalk. The two of them seemed so pleased with each other, I wondered for a minute whether I should just leave them both so that they could continue their fascinating discussion. Obviously, I did nothing of the sort. I mean, I have a knack for saying the wrong thing, and I can also be difficult, but I don't like to make trouble. I stood there frozen and mute seeing how far I could bury my face inside my jacket. I should have just interrupted and sped up the good-byes, because after a few innocent remarks, Grandma decided it would be a great idea to invite Soufi over later for a bite to eat! My God! I thought I would die of embarrassment. Of course, Soufi didn't say no. He looked me up and down with his twinkling eyes, just tickled about the way it had turned out, while that idiot Vincent just stared up at me vacantly.

This explains why I was so happy to be able to get back at Soufi with the blue shadow spell. Ha! That would teach him to get himself invited over and embarrass me right in the middle of the street.

After Operation Blue Shadow, Grandma finally let me out of the cellar. We came back into the daylight and spent the rest of the afternoon normally enough. I played upstairs, going through Grandma's old armoires and discovering all sorts of old things that time had forgotten. Grandma even gave me a couple of very pretty wicker baskets that dated from her wedding.

When snack time came, Soufi turned up as promised. Grandma and I were dying as he told us how he had been "kidnapped." I had to pinch my palms hard under the table to stop myself from laughing, and Grandma bit her tongue and smiled while she stared into her crepe batter. We wolfed down a mountain of sugary crepes.

Then Grandma started reading again, and Soufi and I spent the rest of the afternoon in the attic. I showed him the hidden treasures in the armoires: old clothes, framed photos, frayed straw hats, and the tiny bits and pieces delicately tucked away in shoe boxes—dolls made of seashells, painted eggs, tiny teaspoons with decorated handles...

"You're so lucky," Soufi kept saying. "You're so lucky to have a grandmother and to be able to play around with all this old stuff. Look at this old thing for music! I'm sure if I wind it up, we could listen to a record. There, take one from that pile."

The gramophone still worked, and we listened to a few of the heavy black records. The music crackled, and the high and low pitched voices sang against background melodies that sometimes jumped a few bars. Soufi looked at me and laughed.

"Put that one on again," he said, taking one from the pile.

I was thinking how happy we were, and that we looked just like a young couple from a movie.

Then, sitting cross-legged next to each other on the floor, we read through old comic books, which Grandma had never thrown away, along with all the other books and magazines from when she was a kid. The old paper was soft, and had a good smell.

Soufi and I didn't talk about anything; we just had fun going through stuff. It was really a great afternoon. I wonder why the girls at school make such a big deal about inviting a boy over. You just have to be yourself and act like you always do. There's no point trying to come up with dumb conversations. You just talk if you feel like it and laugh if you want to. If the boy does the same thing, then it's easy to get along well. It's simple.

I thought that Soufi and I got along really well.

3

That night when I got home, I felt confused. It was true that I had really gotten a kick out of the blue shadow episode, and I was excited when I thought about how much fun Soufi and I had had. It was also true that my grandma's crepes were the best ever. But I still had a funny feeling about the day. I guess I was annoyed with Grandma for agreeing with my mother and trying to teach me witchcraft. I preferred her to be completely on my side. I was also worried about what school might be like the next day. I thought that Soufi might make fun of me and my family. After all, even though I'd had so much fun with *him*, I didn't really know if he felt the same way about *me*.

So there I was, sitting at the kitchen table plunged in my dark thoughts when my mom came along and sat down. She sat beside me, eyeing me longingly, as close as a cop handcuffed to a prisoner.

I don't know exactly what she was hoping to hear about my day with Grandma, but I guess she wanted to hear something big! After a few stupid questions, which were crushed by the silence, she tried getting back to the subject of witchcraft.

"So, darling, are we feeling better than we did yesterday?" She had a few more of those typical questions. It made me furious. I got up from the table, and I thought as hard as I could, *Well, since I'm a witch, I wish I could make all the plates in the kitchen fly across the room and smash into a thousand pieces. And I'd like it to happen right this minute, if that's okay.* I slammed the door and went to lock myself in my bedroom. A few seconds later, I heard the most almighty racket. I was sure it was the neighbors bashing on the pipes again.

Just when I thought I had some peace, I heard Mom calling me from the kitchen, sounding really sweet for some reason. Nobody likes to be interrupted during a tantrum, but I had to go see why she was calling. When I got there, the kitchen door was hard to open. Inside the kitchen, the floor was covered with thousands of splinters of china and glass, which had piled up against the bottom of the door. I glanced in through the half-open doorway. I had never seen such destruction in my entire life—not a single glass or plate was still in one piece.

At first, I didn't understand what had happened. I

figured that in one of her fits of fury, my mom had broken all the dishes. But when I saw her smiling face all aglow, and when she began hugging and congratulating me, I realized. It was because of *me* that the dishes had smashed themselves to pieces against the wall. The moment that Mom had always longed for had finally arrived.

In a way, I expected it. I had already gotten used to the idea that it would happen one of these days. It was bound to. But still, faced with the reality of my amazing transformation, I did feel my heart skip a beat. *Well, Verbena,* I said to myself with a burst of pride, *looks like you've earned the right to bust up the china!*

I think that if I had been alone when I found out, I really might have bursted out laughing. But my mother was just so darned pleased with it all that she spoiled the fun. When it came to celebrating, there was only room for one of us. I wasn't interested in sharing her happy moment, nor did I want her sharing mine. This pottery Pearl Harbor should be my little adventure, not hers. I didn't want her butting into my life.

So when she asked me if I had done it all on purpose, I acted dumb. I pretended I'd never asked for anything to happen, and then to really aggravate her, I complained again about what a pain in the butt these "special powers" were going to be for me. I left the kitchen, slamming the door, and thought with all my might: *I want a gust of wind from the heavens to make all these lousy windows start banging open and shut.* When I heard the bangs and crashes coming from the kitchen, I knew it had worked. So it was true—I really was a witch, through and through.

In some ways, it was a curse.

Back in my room again, I sat on my bed and began to think. It seemed a little bit weird that my powers decided to debut on the very same day I'd been visiting with Grandma. I should have been more suspicious of her. Behind her sweet-little-old-lady looks, she was just a witch like all the others—cunning and obstinate—like my mother, like me. I was old enough now to know that you can't trust anybody, least of all your own family.

The sorrier I felt for myself, the more melancholy I became. I imagined my future alone. Was it possible that any normal guy, someone like Soufi, would ever want to marry a girl who could kidnap him with a blue tornado? Would he be able to stand my smashing the dishes at the slightest whim? Would he mind fixing up the cellar so I could store my preserved mandrakes, cages of poison centipedes, and disemboweled bats? Would he be able to deal with the double feature of my mother and my grandma at our wedding? And what would he say the day he found out that his oldest daughter was also a witch? I could smash dishes and bang windows all my life. No normal guy is ever going to ask me to marry him. Not ever! Tears welled up in my eyes. A curse, that's what it was, a real curse!

4

*T*hursday morning at school, I tried to keep out of sight. When I saw Soufi coming toward my part of the playground, I hid. I know it's crazy, but I felt really intimidated. Anyway then the bell rang, and we had to get in line to go into class. As soon as he saw me, Soufi came over.

"Hi, Verbena, you okay?"

"Oh, yeah. I'm fine."

"Well you're lucky because since yesterday, I've been feeling weird."

"You think it's because of my grandma?"

Soufi looked at me wide-eyed and started laughing.

"Oh no, not at all, your grandmother's very nice. It's because..."

I was already shaking because of what he would say when the teacher interrupted our conversation.

"Soufi, stop chatting. It's time for class."

I was so worried, I didn't pay a bit of attention through the first part of the morning. All I did was think about Soufi, turning around in my chair to make sure he was okay. I ended up getting in trouble.

"Verbena!" the teacher shouted. "Stop turning around like that. The class is over here, not behind you. I know that Soufi is very attractive, but he's not the one who's teaching the class!"

Everyone burst out laughing, and I turned bright red. When the bell rang and everyone rushed out for recess, Soufi was waiting for me. I saw one or two kids snickering at us as we went off alone to talk in private. Sometimes I think people are really dumb.

With his hands crossed behind his back, Soufi walked next to me. He kept his eyes to the ground, and he looked very worried.

"I hope you haven't mentioned that weird thing yesterday to anyone."

"Don't worry, I haven't."

"Well, keep it that way. Don't talk about it. I'm scared. I am starting to think that maybe I'm going crazy or maybe I'm getting really sick. Do you think I should see a doctor?"

I knew this was going to happen, and now it really had. The tiniest thing about witchcraft—even something harmless or dumb—attracts trouble, like a moth to a candle flame. Just to impress me, Grandma had ruined my best friend's life. What could I say to the poor guy? Tell him it was completely my fault? That my grandmother thought he was the perfect guinea pig for her stupid experiment? And admit that I'd chosen him as a victim, to get kidnapped in the middle of soccer practice by a phantom tornado? I was so embarrassed, I had no idea what to say.

"I'm sure it's nothing to worry about," I said confidently. "I can guarantee that what happened to you is absolutely not a big deal. You definitely don't need a doctor, and believe me, I know what I'm talking about."

Soufi raised his eyes and looked at me as if it were me who was crazy.

"And what exactly do you know about all this?"

"I know. That's all."

That's how our talk ended, but I could see that despite what I'd said, he didn't believe me. He looked worried all day long.

I hoped that Soufi would become less worried as time went on.

The next morning, I could see that instead, things had gotten worse. I hung around near the front doors to see him arriving. When I finally saw him, I hardly recognized him. Instead of looking like his usual athletic, soccer-player self, his face looked completely exhausted. He was all hunched over, and he actually seemed weighed down by his school bag. Under his dark eyes, he had black rings.

"Feel better?" I asked stupidly.

"Worse is more like it. I didn't sleep all night. Maybe I should tell my mom."

Oh, man. Things had really taken a turn for the worse, and I was starting to feel guiltier and guiltier. I mean, if it hadn't been for me and my wretched family, nothing would have happened to Soufi. All morning, I wondered if I should tell him the truth; I weighed the pros and cons. I didn't listen to my teacher for even a second, and I ended up getting punished. But at lunchtime, I decided I was going to tell Soufi everything, and it was just too bad for Grandma. She should be more careful about who she tries her spells on. The only important thing was to make sure her latest victim would be okay.

I caught up with Soufi outside the cafeteria. I brought him to a quiet spot in the playground, where we sat down leaning up against the wall. Then I told him everything—my mom, my grandma, me, and the blue tornado. He listened to me, openmouthed, not saying a word. When I finished, he gave me a big slap on the leg.

"If any other girl had told me that story, I would

never have believed it. But for some reason, there's something different about you. I believe every word you said."

"You don't think I'm crazy?"

"If one of us is crazy, I'd say it's you. I, myself, am totally normal and sane. And it's a huge relief to know."

"Good. But this time I'm the one asking you not to mention it. Promise not to say a word to anyone! Do you swear?"

He took my hands and held them both. "I swear. Now you have to swear that you will never put another one of those spells on me again. Ever."

"Never. I swear."

We got up to go back to the others.

"Would you like to come over to my grandmother's next Wednesday?"

"Okay," said Soufi, "but maybe you shouldn't tell her you told me everything. We have enough problems..."

That evening I met Soufi's family. I didn't want to seem too eager to go over, but he was the one who insisted.

"Come to my house today," he offered. "My mom will make us a snack, and you can see where I live."

"I don't know if I should," I told him. "I feel kind of shy."

"You should come," Soufi answered back. "After all, I came to your grandmother's and that wasn't so easy."

I didn't want him to think I was pathetic or wimpy, and I just loved the idea that the whole school would see us leaving together and heading off in the same direction. So I said yes, and followed him. I knew my mom wouldn't be home yet, and I had time before she'd start wondering where I was.

His mom was home when we got there—a fifth-floor apartment in a modern building. She was in the kitchen peeling vegetables, her hair covered by a scarf wrapped like a turban around her head. When she saw us, she wiped her hands on her apron and came to say hello. Soufi spoke to her in a language I didn't understand. I think he must have been telling her who I was, because his mother looked over to me and nodded her head from time to time.

When we sat down at the table, the kitchen seemed smaller, and it felt as if we filled up the room. Out the window, we could see trees and other apartment buildings and we could hear birds singing and children coming home from school. Soufi's mom took a plastic box from a cupboard and handed it to Soufi. He put it on the table. It was full of little cookies made with almonds, pistachios, and honey. To be polite, I ate the cookies. But after three, my mouth was full of sugar, and I really didn't feel hungry. When I refused a fourth with a wave of my hand, Soufi's mother laughed and said something to her son.

"My mother thinks you ought to take one or two home with you," he translated. "She says you're as skinny as a blade of grass, and she'd like to fatten you up a bit."

To show my good manners, I nibbled at another cookie. Soufi's kitchen felt nice and warm. I was comfortable there, and would have liked to stay, to help peel the vegetables, wait for the others to come home, and even have dinner, but it was out of the question. I had to go home.

"Do you want to see the apartment?" asked Soufi as I got up to leave.

The living room was decorated with thick rugs overlapping each other on the floor. On the TV were photos of all the children, two boys and three girls, all with brown eyes like Soufi and his mother. In the photo they were on the beach with two older people.

"Are they your grandparents?" I asked Soufi.

"Yeah. Every year my father takes pictures during our vacation in Brittany. When we get home, he sticks the old ones in an album and puts the new ones in the frames."

In the bedrooms there were beds jammed together and shelves full of clothing.

"I sleep with my big brother," said Soufi, pointing to the bunk beds.

Photos of soccer players lined the walls, and pairs of cleats were stacked at the bottom of an armoire.

Soufi is so lucky. His family is huge: five children, a mother *and* a father, and a cousin who sleeps on a mattress in the hallway. Since the apartment is too small for everyone to be inside for long, the kids play in the courtyard of the building. They do lots of things. Soufi swims, plays soccer, and goes to chess club. He even told me he does the shopping for an old lady who lives on the sixth floor.

When I left the apartment, Soufi's mother handed me two cookies wrapped in a piece of plastic wrap. I wanted to kiss her good-bye, but I didn't dare. I just shook her hand, and she put her hand on her heart. I ate the cookies on the way home. I thought I was going to choke, I was so stuffed, but I didn't want to take them into my house. I would have to explain to my mom where they had come from. Mom would definitely have seen it as an opportunity to try to get to meet Soufi and his family, to get to know his mother, and to see his apartment. No way! I'd rather die choking on almond cookies.

5

The following Wednesday I didn't really feel like seeing Grandma. I was mad at her. I couldn't stop thinking it was her fault I had changed so suddenly and so completely. And I was worried about what was going to happen next.

But the last thing I wanted was to spend the whole day with my mom. So I woke up very early, got ready as quietly as I could so as not to wake Mom, and when Grandma came to pick me up, I followed her out the door as if nothing had happened. As for Grandma, she must have been feeling slightly self-conscious. We had hardly got out the door when she started telling me she had had absolutely nothing to do with what had happened, that she thought I was a bit young for this witchcraft business, and she didn't agree with my mother. All of her excuses made it obvious—she was feeling guilty. I took this little speech as an apology, and I decided to let it go. After all, it was going to happen one day, so what difference did it make if it happened sooner rather than later? Besides, telling Soufi all our family secrets had somehow taken a load off my mind.

We spent the morning gardening. I like helping Grandma when she's working in the garden. I'm happy to concentrate on cleaning up the flower beds, trimming the lawn, or pruning the bushes.

We were both bent over the ground with our noses next to the soil when Grandma asked me what trick I would like to learn first, now that I was a witch.

Actually, I hadn't really thought about it. And yet, I did have an idea, which came all by itself—as if it had been sitting there in my head for a long time just waiting to be asked to be let out.

"I want to find my father," I said.

As soon as the words had flown out of my mouth, I thought finally I had said exactly and precisely what I was thinking. To find my father was what I wanted to do for sure. Grandma protested a little bit—just because she knew she should—but I think what really concerned her was the way my mother might react. Deep down she must have agreed with me because she ended up saying that since she couldn't stop me, she would help me.

"Right now?" I asked.

"Right now," she agreed.

And we went on with our weeding.

At lunchtime, Grandma got out her fryer and peeled some potatoes. I cut them with a special machine that transforms a potato into about fifteen fries in a split second.

The oil was simmering over the flame. Grandma threw in a bulb of garlic, to give it flavor, and then lowered the french fries into their boiling bath. She always does french fries twice so they'll be crisp on the outside and soft inside. When they were ready, Grandma made a couple of paper cones out of thick blue paper and filled them up to the brim.

On the table were vinegar, pickles, and mayonnaise.

"Sit down, darling," she said, handing me my cone, "and tell me about your week."

Picking at the french fries, I began to tell her about my classes, my teachers, my friends, and about Soufi. One thing led to another, and I got so carried away by my story, I ended up telling her everything without realizing what a traitor I was being.

"So I told him it was you who had made the blue shadow and he shouldn't worry."

Suddenly Grandma raised her eyes from her french fries, but I went on and on enthusiastically.

"I also told him that we were all witches in the family—you, me, Mom. He was really glad I told him."

Grandma shook her head and tapped her finger against her temple several times.

"So he was happy, was he? And he'll have nothing better to do than shout it from the rooftops for everyone to hear. And that's when trouble will come down on us like a plague of locusts. It's because of big mouths like you that for centuries witches have been burned."

My usually understanding grandma didn't look so understanding anymore. She looked really mad. My throat tightened, and I felt like crying.

"He promised he wouldn't say a word."

"Well, that is just marvelous!"

"And anyway, no one would believe him!"

Grandma raised her eyebrows. "That's the only chance we have, you ninny! These days, people no longer believe in witches. That's the only reason they have stopped burning them—because they don't see them anymore. Nowadays, when people around town want someone to take out their frustrations on, they prefer to take it out on poor immigrants—they're easier to spot than witches. But remember! If one day our neighbors start believing in witchcraft again, you'll have to be more careful! We'll immediately be labeled as fair game; we'll be burned on any pretext: drought, floods, flu epidemic, or stock market crash!"

I hung my head in shame.

"But Soufi isn't like just any old neighbor," I murmured. "First of all, he's an immigrant himself. His family comes from some other place, and his mother doesn't even speak French..."

"Well," said Grandma resignedly, "it's too late now. The damage is done. The only thing we can do is trust Soufi and hope he keeps his mouth shut."

*G*randma took off her apron while I quietly cleared the table.

"We're not going to sit here all afternoon worrying about it," she said with a conciliatory smile. "We have more important things to do."

"Good," I told her. "So you're not mad?"

"I'm much too nice to stay in a bad mood for long."

"So are we going to find my dad?"

"Well, first I have to look for my liquid mirror," said Grandma. "I lent it to that crazy old Aselmina one day when she lost her keys. I'll have to go find her and get it back."

"And what about me?"

"You can wait for me at Madame Arsène's. I don't like leaving you all alone in the house. I'll pick you up on my way back. I won't be long."

Since I was little I'd always gone to Madame Arsène's by climbing over the wall and sliding down the other side.

I went to the shed to get the ladder. Grandma won't let me climb up the pear trees anymore; she says I'm too heavy, and I'll end up breaking one of the branches. That's bad for the pear tree and for me, too, because I'd crash right down to the ground. I climbed over the tiles on top of the wall and dropped gently down onto the gravel path in Madame Arsène's garden. I made my way across the garden through her lettuce patch and raspberry bushes, and I pushed open the kitchen door. Madame Arsène was putting out crumbs for the sparrows.

"Hello, my little kitten," she said, as she always does whenever she sees me come through the kitchen door.

"Hello, Madame Arsène. Can I stay with you for half an hour? Grandma had to go out."

"Sit down and take a cookie."

I gobbled down a few cookies while Madame Arsène sprinkled the windowsill with crumbs. She added a few little bits of butter and a bowl of water for the birds to drink, then she sat down opposite me.

"So, Madame Arsène," I asked, "I heard that you knew my grandfather?"

She nodded her head.

"Oh, what a handsome man, believe me. You could

say he made a perfect match with your grandmother. They were both tall and kind and full of life."

"What did he do? Was he a magician?"

"Gervais, a magician? Heavens no! He was a florist. He worked in the greenhouses; he was an orchid specialist. But he didn't only know about orchids, and he didn't just have a green thumb, you know. He had green arms! Oh, your grandmother was so happy. Not for long enough, that's true, but she was very happy indeed. Not like me and Maurice. Gervais died too young. But not my Maurice; Maurice is still with us..."

I didn't want Madame Arsène to start complaining about her husband. Once she started, she didn't stop. I listened to her to be polite, but I was feeling really embarrassed. To interrupt her, I asked, "What did he die of?"

"But I just told you, Maurice is not dead..."

"No, I mean Gervais."

"Didn't your grandmother tell you? He died from pricking himself on a rose. The thorn went in deep and got infected. It infected his finger, then his arm, then his heart. Your grandmother tried everything in her power, but she couldn't change his destiny. The poor woman found herself all alone with your mother. My Maurice would never even have the chance to get pricked by a rose, I can tell you. He has never even once given me a bouquet of flowers—not once in his whole life."

Luckily, Grandma rang the doorbell and put an end to Madame Arsène's gripe session.

"Come sit down and have a few cookies with us," she suggested to Grandma.

But Grandma refused.

"Sorry. We have a guest waiting for us in front of the house," she said. "We have to get home. Good-bye."

"Good-bye," echoed Madame Arsène from where she stood on her doorstep.

PART 4

What Soufi Thought

(A boy's voice)

1

At the beginning of the year, I hadn't noticed her. She was pretty low-key, the type of girl you think of as one of those "good students" and forget about. She had no brothers or sisters at school. I'm saying that because I have three siblings between first and fifth grade. The other thing I noticed was that her parents were never waiting for her outside school, not even on Saturday mornings, when most parents are free to pick up their kids from class.

She had friends. At recess, the girls always hung out in groups of four or five. But she never invited any of them home. And the boys in the class? She just wasn't interested. If I hadn't seen her laughing with the other girls and looking our way, I'd have figured that she didn't even notice us.

But I certainly noticed her. First, because of her name. I had already met lots of Roses, Violets, and Lilys.

But this was the first time I had ever encountered a Verbena! Then, I noticed her because she had this look. One morning in gym, her look just struck me like lightning.

"Wow," I said to myself, "she looks so much like someone I know, but who is it?"

I stood there awhile watching her run, but I just couldn't remember who she reminded me of. At lunchtime in the cafeteria, I followed her with my tray and sat at her table.

"Verbena, you look just like someone I know."

"Oh yeah? Who?"

"That's the problem. I don't know..."

"That's interesting..."

She acted like she didn't care, but I could tell by her sly smile she was glad I'd sat with her. Celine, who was sitting next to her, gaped at me like a fish, trying to get my attention. The whole class knows that Celine totally loves me. Too bad I don't feel the same way. My type is more like Verbena. Someone a little bit more serious but with a sense of humor; someone a bit mysterious, I suppose.

For a few days, my search for who she looked like seemed to amuse Verbena, but then I realized she was getting fed up with it. She never smiled at me anymore. She ignored me.

"You just invented the whole thing to be funny," she accused.

I denied it, but she didn't want to hear anything I said. Now she couldn't even stand me. It was really depressing. But I wasn't going to give up, so I kept on trying to figure out who she looked like. One day, I even asked the school guard if he had any idea, but he didn't have a clue. I tried to figure it out by process of elimination: it couldn't be anyone in her family, because I don't know her family. It couldn't be anyone at school, or the guard would have noticed. So who was it? Not knowing was driving me crazy.

From the very first day I noticed her, Verbena became part of my life. She didn't do it on purpose—I know that's true. But the way things worked out, we became sort of inseparable. One day, because of a huge coincidence, her grandmother invited me over for crepes. Yeah, her *grandmother* invited me! I was on my way to soccer with Vincent, when we ran into Verbena and her grandmother in the street. The grandmother was dressed in an enormous sort of red velvet outfit—it was unbelievable how she stuck out. Verbena was holding her hand like a little elf attached to a giant troll. Inside, I was dying of laughter—but I kept a straight face. I didn't want to seem rude in front of her grandmother.

As they went past us, I said hello loudly, and Verbena hardly answered. But her grandmother immediately got into a conversation with us. She seemed so nice that we just kept on talking—right there in the street. Verbena looked as if she wished she were dead. She didn't even open her mouth. Anyway, in the end, her grandmother asked us if we wanted to go and have crepes with them after soccer. I honestly thought Verbena would faint. I accepted the invitation, half to be polite, and half to annoy Verbena. If I had known how she would take her revenge, I wouldn't have risked it; I would have said no. But luckily, *I* can't see into the future!

2

The next thing that happened was that Verbena bewitched me. It may seem totally insane, but it's the whole truth. Really and truly. In fact, Verbena is actually a witch. Poor little witch girl...it's not her fault; her mother and grandmother are witches, too. She told me herself, and I know what I'm talking about, because I actually experienced her magical powers.

That Wednesday morning when I told her grandmother I'd come for crepes, I unknowingly walked into a family of witches. And they had nothing better to do than cast a spell on me...right in the middle of my soccer practice. I mean, for a guy like me, who loves soccer, it's not the kind of thing you would forget. Verbena explained later that her grandmother had cooked up this spell in her cellar, and that once it was ready to go, it had to be cast on someone. Verbena just threw out my name.

And that's how I, the innocent bystander, found myself caught up in this whirlwind!

This all happened during a scrimmage game against another school. There I was, sitting quietly on the sidelines, when this sort of tornado drove straight down the field toward me. *Wow, what's that?* I thought. *It's heading straight for me!* I tried to get up, but I couldn't—I was glued to the bench. I wanted to yell, but I couldn't make a sound. Two seconds later, this tornado thing was right in front of me, and it sucked me in! Soon I was inside of it. And it was like paradise or something, like blue cotton candy, soft and comfortable. I felt like I was in a dream. But it didn't last long.

All of a sudden, I found myself sitting in the mud and on the other end of the field in front of this idiot Kevin. The tornado spat me out like a piece of rotten fruit.

Aside from Kevin, the stupidest guy on earth, nobody had just seen what had happened to me. I didn't want people to think I was nuts, so I just kept to myself, saying nothing, and went back to sit on my bench. And that's when I started to worry.

That afternoon at Anastabotte's (Verbena's grandmother), I was so blown away that I told them the whole story. I guess I really trusted them. They seemed so honest, the two of them cooking crepes side by side in that cozy kitchen. What a couple of double-crossers.

Obviously, they didn't think anything of it. To hear them, you'd have thought everyone traveled from one end of a soccer field to the other in a blue tornado. I should have been more careful, but I was so glad that Verbena's grandma had invited me over, and I was just so happy about spending the afternoon with her. While Anastabotte did the dishes we went up to the attic. I got this gramophone to work, and we listened to antique 78's. Then we looked at some old comic books, and Verbena showed me a bunch of amazing things that her grandmother has kept around to remind her of her youth.

It's hard for me to explain why I think that afternoon I spent in the attic was so much fun. Maybe it's because attics are romantic, but maybe it's because I was alone with Verbena. I didn't even need to look at her to feel happy. Whatever she did, she did well; whatever she said was funny. With her, the slightest thing became interesting. The whole time we were in the attic, I didn't think once about the tornado.

It was when I left Anastabotte's that I remembered my weird adventure. The memory wouldn't leave my mind. In the end, it took over all the space I had, and by the time I got home, I was terrified.

I said nothing to my parents. They wouldn't have listened, and if by any remote chance my mother had believed me, she would have been so worried that she'd never have let me go to soccer again. The only way I managed to get to sleep that night was because my brother sleeps in the same room. The sound of his snoring relaxed me.

The following day, I still felt scared. And if the day was bad, the night was totally awful. I lay there with my teeth chattering until dawn. I could see myself surrounded by evil spirits, and I was convinced I was going crazy and I'd be shut up in a mental institution.

At school, everyone noticed that I wasn't myself. I was in such bad shape, even Verbena (who was behind it all) felt sorry for me. To make me feel better, she confessed everything. If I hadn't been sure she was telling the truth, I would have laughed in her face. But I knew she wasn't lying. If she had made it up, how could she have known so much about what happened to me? I might have hated her for playing such a dirty trick on me, but after she had finished explaining, I was so grateful that I just wanted to give her a big hug. I thought it was really brave of her to trust me with all her personal secrets. After all, who was I to her? She could have turned me into a beetle with a wave of her hand, but no, she decided to share her secret with me. What a great girl! She might be a double-crosser, but she's still awesome!

That evening, I took her home to my apartment. It

was my way of saying thank you. I introduced her to my mother and showed her around. Now that I knew about her grandmother and her secret, I wanted her to know something about my life, too. I showed her my soccer cleats and gave her some of my mother's almond cookies. She seemed happy having tea with us in our little kitchen, and I was glad.

"What do you think of her?" I asked my mother when Verbena had left.

"She seems nice," said Mom, putting away the cookies on the top shelf of the cupboard. "She's pretty."

"Is that all?"

Mom laughed. "I think that you like her. That's what I think."

She was right, as usual.

3

The rest of the week I looked at Verbena with new appreciation. Whenever our eyes met, I thought how lucky I was. This girl, who could do so many incredible things, was taking the time to smile at me. An adorable wink from her, and I had to pinch myself to make sure it was real. On Saturday afternoon, I went to soccer again, feeling slightly nervous. At lunchtime, I asked her, "Are you going to your grandmother's again this afternoon?"

"No. Why?"

"Because I have soccer practice. So I just thought I'd let you know. I'd rather you didn't put any spells on me while I'm playing."

Verbena cracked up, and the delicious sound of her laughter rushed over me like a waterfall.

"I've already promised myself never to put a spell on you again. Anyway, the truth is I don't like doing witchcraft. I don't have a choice about having these powers—I'm stuck with them—but I don't want to bother anyone with them, either. Don't worry, go on ahead. You can trust me."

Of course I trusted her. I didn't have much choice, did I?

The following Wednesday, Verbena invited me over again. I have to admit, I was a bit anxious about going back to the old witch's house. But I wanted to see that little garden again, and to be alone with Verbena in the attic.

After soccer, I raced over to her grandmother's and rang the doorbell. It was five o'clock. I was waiting for them to answer the door like normal people do, when I saw them both come out of the neighbor's house. The neighbor had a wrinkled face and looked pretty much like a witch herself. I saw her gazing nastily at me from her doorway.

"Hello, Soufi," said the grandmother, getting a key from her pocket. "Word has it that you now know a little something about our family?"

"Yeah, I guess so," I mumbled, scared out of my wits.

I glanced at Verbena, who nodded vigorously. So that was it! She had told her grandmother everything. This girl killed me. Was she not scared for me or for herself? I just hoped the grandmother hadn't decided to fatten me up and have me for supper. And I hoped she wasn't planning on turning me into a pillar of salt. Or a canary in a cage!

"I hope you're not angry," I said, turning toward Anastabotte, sounding pathetic.

Anastabotte grimaced. "If it were up to me, I wouldn't mind cooking you up one of my little surprises to keep you quiet, but since it was my granddaughter who decided to let you in on the secret, I'll let it go. She's old enough to know what she's doing."

Phew! The two witches went into the kitchen. Anastabotte set a heavy-looking bag down on the table.

"Careful, don't break it," whispered Verbena.

The grandmother turned toward me with the piercing stare of a cannibal. Then she looked at her granddaughter with a mysterious smile. I felt sick to my stomach. What was I doing with these twisted maniacs? Why wasn't I at home with my sweet wonderful mother, breathing in the smell of warm cookies?

"We've got work to do." Anastabotte grinned enthusiastically.

"Important work," added Verbena, who suddenly seemed very excited.

I thought I'd better leave. I was about to tell them, but the words lingered too long inside my head, and I never got them out.

"Er, um," I stammered, "Maybe I . . . ."

"Since this young man already knows about us, he can stay. He'll see a few things he didn't bargain for." Anastabotte's verdict was final. She stabbed me with a piercing look that nailed me in place.

"Okay, he'll stay," agreed Verbena, without asking my opinion. There it was. My fate was sealed. They must have already discussed it behind my back. I was probably about to live the last hours of my brief existence. I was about to pay for my mistakes. I wanted to scream and run away, but I was too terrified to do anything. I stood there frozen in silence. Before my horrified eyes, the grandmother opened a drawer and took out a bunch of rusty keys.

"Let's go down to the cellar," she said.

I felt my knees buckling.

In a motion that reminded me of a garbage collector, Anastabotte grabbed her heavy bag from the counter and added, "Give your friend a glass of water. He doesn't look so good. I'll take the liquid mirror."

Verbena handed me a glass of water. I sipped it like a condemned man, forcing myself to taste every drop since it was the last drink of my life . . .

Then we went down to the cellar.

4

That cellar! It was black as night, dusty, dirty, and it stank of formaldehyde and rotten vegetables. It looked like a garbage dump, but one set up by a crazy person. Shapeless things hung from the walls, weird looking pieces of unidentifiable something-or-other floated in old jelly jars lined up on the shelves. In the middle of this horrifying mess, a collection of old pots and pans were rotting away. And yet Verbena, my friend who always came across as such a neat freak, seemed totally at home here. She bounced around from shelf to shelf, chatting away, happy to show me everything while I made a superhuman effort not to pass out!

"You see that?" she said, pointing at a jar full of roots. "Those are mandrakes—very important for making the blue shadow... and over there..."

"Please don't. I'd rather not know," I muttered.

"Are you angry?" she asked, looking up at me innocently.

Then it was Anastabotte's turn. She came up and scrutinized me, both her eyes riveted on mine. I swayed, closed my eyes, and prepared to breathe my last breath. After a moment, she said to her granddaughter, "Do you realize that the poor dear is absolutely terrified?"

"Is that true, Soufi? You're scared?"

Verbena was making fun of me. That was the final humiliation, and it made me feel even worse.

"I thought you'd like to see Grandma's workshop! It's not every day that you get to see a witch in action. Even better, we're going to do the coolest spell. I wanted you to see it..."

"Ha, ha," I croaked. "I'm not the least bit scared. Just push that stool toward me, will you? I'm feeling sort of weak. Soccer practice kills me. Now, what's this spell?"

Verbena looked questioningly at her grandmother and said, "I'm going to try to find my dad."

Huh? What did she say? Trying to find her dad? When I think that she could be doing a spell to find a winning lottery ticket—or anything else she wants! But no—she'd rather try and find her father, a guy who she's never even seen. What a girl! What an unbelievable girl. I mean, I really felt kind of honored that she had invited me along. I breathed a big sigh of relief. Another guy might have been frightened in my position, but I'm no coward. I like discovering new things. I love taking a risk!

"Great," I said, hoping I sounded enthusiastic.

To tell you the truth, I think I more or less shouted out, "You are so awesome!"

I wanted to run over to her and grab her and cover her face with kisses, like in the movies. But I didn't. Some other time maybe, when her grandmother isn't around. A few weeks from now, far away from this cellar, I could do it. Maybe. It takes the right set of circumstances and a certain amount of courage to cover a girl's face in kisses, even if that's how they do it in movies. In movies, everything always seems so simple.

While I was dreaming secretly of covering her granddaughter with kisses, Anastabotte opened up her bag. Like a mom carefully picking up a tiny baby, she took out a sort of huge golden salad bowl that had a layer of white jelly trembling at the bottom. Excuse the gruesome comparison, but it looked like an eye. A huge blind eye shining up at you from the bottom of a dish.

"Ugh!" I said.

"Wow!" Verbena contributed.

"Watch out, kids," Anastabotte replied.

She put the bowl on a table. The three of us

approached and stared at the eye. The jelly misted over under the gaze of our six eyeballs.

"My God in Heaven!" said Anastabotte. "Looks like we're going to have some fun, my little sorcerer's apprentices! Verbena, listen to me. I'm going to say a spell. It's long, but you have to repeat it after me. Make sure you repeat every single syllable, otherwise we won't get anywhere and the liquid mirror will be spoiled. As for you, Soufi, try to empty your mind. If you think too hard, your thoughts will get mixed up with ours. Are you ready?"

My throat was tight with emotion, and I nodded my head. Verbena's face was expressionless. She was totally focused on her orders. She already looked spellbound.

"Good," said Anastabotte. "Let's all try and focus for a few minutes, and we'll get this thing going." She took a deep breath of the stinky, disgusting air and started to chant some sort of prayer in a language I had never heard before, where the syllables *oum*, *bot*, and *dad* came up over and over. Verbena repeated after her. Their voices rose higher and higher, and the echo was so loud, I thought my eardrums would burst. Soon, with their eyes half closed, their hands shaking, and their faces chalky white, they were chanting (and almost shouting!) at the tops of their lungs. I tried my best to keep my head as empty as a drum and stared nonstop into the white jelly at the bottom of the bowl.

As their voices grew louder, I could see gray shadows gliding into the eye's gelatinous mass. At first, I couldn't see anything specific, just shadowy lines making stripes across the white background. Then, little by little, the gray lines came together until a shape appeared. Wow! I began to get all jittery. The two witches went on chanting for a while, and the shapes in the bowl grew more distinct. Now, traced in the jelly, I could clearly see a picture of a man running. He was dressed in a sweat suit and a baseball cap.

"That's it!" cried Anastabotte suddenly. Look in the mirror, Verbena! He's there!"

I jumped, and Verbena came out of her trance. She lowered her eyes and looked hard into the bowl.

"That's him," Anastabotte whispered. "That's your father."

"Unbelievable," said Verbena in a low voice, "that's my father."

Then she raised her head, disappointed.

"But I don't even know this guy. Who is he?" she asked.

"That's another story," said Anastabotte, looking helpless. "I'm just glad that my liquid mirror still works!"

"Sure, but I feel kind of dumb. Going to all this trouble, just to see a guy running . . . and I don't even know who he is!"

As for me, I also took a look at the guy who was running. His baseball cap looked vaguely familiar. Then I looked at Verbena. Then I looked at the guy. Then I looked at Verbena. Then I looked at the cap. Then it hit me. I jumped up and down and yelled out: "Gerald!"

"What about Gerald?" screamed Anastabotte.

"Well, it's Gerald! My soccer coach! He's your father!" Verbena's voice rose and echoed round the cellar.

"Really? My father is the soccer coach? Wow. I wonder what my mom will say..."

That was who she looked like this whole time: like father like daughter—Verbena and the coach. Never in a million years would I have linked these two together. But that mirror put the two of them together. I grabbed Verbena's hand and started dancing her around in the middle of all the rotting pots and pans.

Meanwhile, Anastabotte stared anxiously into her jelly.

"Gerald is the soccer coach? Well, that certainly takes the cake! I knew Gerald, but I had no idea he had become the soccer coach!"

She stuffed her liquid mirror into her bag and turned toward us with an exasperated frown.

"As for you, Soufi, would you kindly stop kissing my granddaughter right this minute! I have already had enough problems today!"

"Why is your grandmother being so serious all of a sudden," I whispered into Verbena's ear.

"Don't let it bother you," said Verbena, giving me a big hug. "She just gets emotional, that's all."

5

We went back up into the daylight. Outside, the garden was bright and sunny. Verbena was happily laughing, and so was I. Even Anastabotte seemed to have forgotten what was bothering her. She disappeared into the kitchen, held up the frying pan like a general, and ordered: "Crepes for everyone!"

The butter sizzled, the batter crisped, and the crepes flew through the air. We got out the sugar and jam. I tied a napkin round my neck, and we started eating. When we were all sitting around the table, Anastabotte looked silently at Verbena for a while. Then, she took a handkerchief from her pocket and wiped her eyes.

"Sweetheart," she said, "I wasn't sure how you'd do just now, downstairs. I was worried. I thought you might be disappointed, and I thought you might spoil my liquid mirror. But now I've seen with my own eyes—you've really got what it takes. You have the willpower, the concentration, and the talent to succeed in anything you want. Thank God," she added almost under her breath.

I was proud of Verbena, too, and I would have liked to make a little speech, but my mouth was full of crepe. Then Anastabotte turned to me.

"Soufi, my boy, Verbena had the brilliant intuition to invite you here today and bring you downstairs while we did the spell. Without you, we would have had a face without the name or address. I would never have recognized Gerald after all these years! I think we should be grateful for your help. You've played quite an important role here today in making Verbena's wish come true. So, thank you. But listen here, my boy, don't you dare get it into your head to shout everything you've seen from the rooftops. Got it?" She stared at me, her eyes wide with worry.

"Madame Anastabotte," I began, "I will do exactly as you tell me. Please trust me."

"So polite!" said Anastabotte, laughing. "Here, have another crepe. You've certainly earned it!"

I was experiencing the kind of satisfaction that a guy can only know stuffing himself with crepes after an afternoon full of emotions. But then I noticed Verbena fidgeting on her chair.

"So? Aren't we going to go find him?" she finally asked, sounding quite exasperated.

"Find who?"

"My dad, of course! Now that I've seen him, I'm not about to let him get away a second time."

"Do you know where we might find him, Soufi?" asked Anastabotte.

"Well, a little while ago he was jogging. After that, I guess he went home."

"Do you know where he lives?"

"Sure. His apartment is near the soccer field."

Verbena suddenly turned pale. She grabbed my hand and quickly asked me, "Is he married? Does he have other children? Another daughter?"

"I warned you, didn't I, darling?" interrupted Anastabotte seriously. "When you turn up in people's lives after eleven years, you may be in for all sorts of surprises."

I tried to remember, but I couldn't remember ever having seen Gerald with a family. Even when we played away games, even when there were team dinners or end of year parties, he was always alone. I had noticed a woman was sometimes waiting for him at the entrance to the stadium after practice, but she never had kids with her. And anyway, she drove her own car. Probably just a girlfriend. A minor girlfriend.

"Well, why don't we go and see him?" said Verbena. "Then at least we'll know."

Anastabotte got up from the table.

"In that case, I'm going to put on some makeup. I don't want to look like I just got out of bed."

"Not too much lipstick, okay, Grandma?" suggested Verbena gently.

We jumped into Anastabotte's car. I sat in the front seat to show her the way, and I found the apartment block easily. We left the car double-parked. I rang the buzzer, and he answered.

"Gerald, it's Soufi."

"Soufi? What brings you here at this hour, kiddo?"

"A surprise."

"I hope it's a good one. Come up. I'm on the fifth floor."

When he opened the door, he saw the three of us. First seeing me, he looked intrigued. Then his eyes took in Verbena. He raked his hair with his hand, then scratched his head, his neck, his stomach, and finally his chin. Then he looked at Anastabotte, who was standing behind us, a quiet smile glowing on her made-up face. That's when he began to understand, and his eyes popped out of his head.

"Anastabotte?"

"Yes, Gerald, it's me."

"Then, then...," he stuttered, looking again at Verbena.

"Yes, it's her," said Anastabotte, putting her hand on Verbena's shoulder.

"I'm Verbena," said Verbena

"Oh my God," said Gerald. "Talk about a surprise!"

And he fainted.

6

Half an hour later, the doctor arrived. Gerald had come to and wanted to stand, but Anastabotte had pressed him down with her hand against his chest.

When he had fainted on his doorstep, she dragged him by the shoulders to the living room couch. Once he was lying on the couch, she had slapped him vigorously to get him to wake up. During this time, Verbena inspected the apartment to make sure there wasn't a kid's bedroom— especially not one belonging to an eleven-year-old girl.

"Stay where you are, my friend," repeated Anastabotte, still pinning Gerald down firmly. "First let's hear what the doctor has to say."

"Nothing, it's nothing at all," said the doctor. "Maybe a lack of magnesium or potassium, but otherwise, you're in excellent shape. Good for you. How would you like to pay?"

"There we go," said Gerald, jumping up from the couch. "I am once again among the living. Pass me my checkbook, will you?"

He served us lemonade and cookies. Then he and Anastabotte sat in the kitchen and chatted for a while. We just sat side by side on the couch with our lemonade.

"He lives alone," said Verbena, sipping quietly. "No trace of a woman in the house, no kid, and no girl. Just sports stuff, books, a mess. That's all."

"I told you, didn't I?"

"I know, but I still had to check. Do you think I should try out for the soccer team?"

"Why not?"

When Gerald and Anastabotte finally came out of the kitchen, they both seemed so happy. Gerald had his arm round Anastabotte, and she was whispering into his ear.

"I've been talking to your dad," Anastabotte said.

"My dad! My dad!" repeated Verbena, feeling the thrill.

"We've decided we have to tell Soufi about our reunion."

"Yeah, yeah," said Verbena, fidgeting.

"I'd like to have you come over on the weekends, take you to the movies, or away for the weekend. To do that, things have to be on the up-and-up with your mother," explained Gerald.

I noticed how well Gerald was handling everything. You could immediately see he was a sportsman: cool, quick reactions, sense of teamwork and fair play. Here was a guy who just an hour ago had been alone in life. Now he was juggling a daughter and her grandma like he'd been doing it all his life. What a champ.

"Everyone in the van," he ordered. "I'm taking Verbena back to her mother's."

"What about my car?" asked Anastabotte.

"I'll bring you back later. But for now, I'd like it if you'd come with us."

Anastabotte stalled.

"Wait half a minute. Let me put on a bit of lipstick."

"Not too much, Grandma, don't overdo it," said Verbena, picking up her jacket.

I got into the back of the van with Verbena, and that's when I realized what a strange thing family resemblance can be. Now that I had both the father and the daughter in front of me, they didn't seem so much alike. Their eyes were different, and their hair wasn't the same color. So what was it? Was it something about the way they smiled, a way of asking questions with their eyes or standing with their hands in their pockets? It's insane how people who look alike can be the same and yet completely different. That's what I was thinking of when I stared at Verbena as hard as I could.

PART 5
....

What Ursula Thought

(A mother's conclusion)

I knew it. I knew I should never have let my mother watch Verbena. She let herself be brainwashed. Who can you trust if not your own mother? You can't trust anyone.

It was the end of a lovely Wednesday. I was quietly reading the paper, a pizza was cooking in the oven, and I had spent half the day in a café with some old girl-friends. We had exchanged recipes and our most bitter feelings about the world. There I was, waiting for my daughter to arrive from her grandmother's, where I was sure she had spent the day making progress on her witch-craft. After all, I had had a phone call from my friend Anselmina earlier in the afternoon.

"Your mother came by to fetch her liquid mirror just now. Looks like she's getting back in the swing of things. Any idea what she's up to?"

"She's giving my daughter private lessons. She probably wants to demonstrate something for her. It's nothing to worry about, believe me."

Just before eight, the doorbell rang. They were back. I got up without even taking off my apron and slowly walked to the front door. I opened it.

"AAAAAAH!!!!"

There were four of them facing me: my daughter, my mother, some good-for-nothing kid from who knows where. And Gerald. Gerald? Where did he come from? I slammed the door. *Bam.* And I leaned against the door handle while my legs turned to jelly. I trusted them, and this is what they did? This is how they made use of their afternoon with the liquid mirror? The one guy I thought I'd managed to shake off for good, and they'd managed to find him. Those witches!

"Mom, it's me, Verbena. Open up."

What could I do? I had no choice. I opened up.

"Hello, Gerald," I said unenthusiastically.

"Hello, Ursula," he said in a similar tone. "It sure is something to see you again after all this time."

And there I was, walking around in my apron without a scrap of makeup, hair only held back by Verbena's hair clip. I couldn't begin to imagine what I must have looked like. If only they'd thought to warn me, at least I could have put on clean clothes!

"Verbena and Anastabotte came to my apartment looking for me," said Gerald. "I suggested taking them home—I thought it'd be safer, and that it'd give me an opportunity to say hi to you."

"Is that so?"

"Still in the same business?"

"Yes, what about you?"

"Oh me? Nothing special."

It was strange. No reproaches. No shouting. Gerald didn't seem furious at all, and I couldn't see any *Ursulacidal* thoughts in his expression. It was as if we had seen each other the night before.

"Can I come in for five minutes?"

"Why?"

"To talk about Verbena, maybe have a drink, even to eat dinner if you invite me."

He came in...followed by Anastabotte, the young boy, and my daughter. I gave them a drink.

Then Gerald called Soufi's parents, and I kept the kids for dinner. Apparently, there's plenty to talk about when you haven't seen someone for eleven years! We talked a lot, mostly about Verbena. Gerald wanted to share the responsibilities of raising her. He would watch her every other weekend and during the holidays. I didn't say no. I figured it wouldn't hurt to take a weekend off from time to time. I would be able to go to the beach with Anselmina. And that way, Verbena would always have a dad to take her to the movies and to restaurants. She couldn't drive me crazy anymore—it would be the end of her complaints!

Throughout the conversation, this Soufi didn't say a word. He just kept his eyes on Verbena. He didn't seem as stupid as Verbena had described. She always exaggerates. He looks like he comes from a nice family, and I think he's a bit ga-ga about my daughter. But however nice I think he is, I'll keep my eye on him.

It was pitch black outside when our guests left. We saw them to the door, and standing outside in the cold night air, Verbena raised her hands up to the sky.

"Look up there," she said.

A shower of green fireworks lit up the sky.

"Not bad," said Anastabotte. "My turn now." It's unbelievable how she always has to show off, even at her age. She never changes! So she raised her arms as well, and a shower of golden light lit up the sky. I didn't want to be left out, it would have looked like I was sulking, so I did my best to throw a wreath of multicolored rockets into the night.

"You haven't lost your touch," Gerald told me.

I was glad to hear it.

"And your daughter's just like you. I mean, she's like both of you," he corrected, turning toward Anastabotte.

"Like mothers like daughters," Anastabotte added. "Enough childishness. Come on, Gerald. Take us home. It's getting late."

Soufi kissed Verbena on the cheek—a bit too close to the mouth, if you ask me. Yes, indeed, I'd better watch him. As my mother would say, "There's a time for everything." Gerald lifted Verbena off the ground and hugged her against him. Anastabotte gave her a wink, and the three of them went off in the van.

All in all, it was a very good evening. I wonder when I will see Gerald again. Probably next Saturday.

The van turned the street corner, and we went inside. I closed the door behind us. Then my daughter threw her arms round my neck and kissed me.

"Mom, I adore you."

I was so pleased that I didn't even answer her. I would rather keep my happiness to myself, in the silence of my heart. We cleared the table, and Verbena got into her pajamas. She was about to go to bed when I said, "By the way, I forgot to ask your father. What does he do for a living these days?"

Verbena chuckled.

"Actually, Mom, he's the soccer coach."

Soccer? Phooey! I guess nothing's perfect!